What People Are Saying About

Feng Shui Your Way to Abundance

I've long believed creating the right work environment is crucial to feeling creative and inspired. I think the same is true for our homes. You know how some places, rooms and homes just have an energy about them. It affects how we think, feel and work. Janine Lowe is an expert in how to do this in a really simple and practical way, and this book is a fabulous resource for others interested in doing this in their own environments.

Shaa Wasmund MBE, Author, Educator, Changemaker; *Sunday Times* Top 20 Most Influential Entrepreneurs in the UK

I used to think Feng Shui was all about keeping the under your bed clear and clean and wearing a particular colour, but after meeting Janine, I realize it is so much more deeper than that. It's about understanding that your home has an energy and that energy isn't flat—it's constantly shifting and it has profound impact on your day-to-day well-being and mood. Whenever I make big decisions such as moving house, I always trust Janine will give me the best advice that will bring the most prosperity and happiness. The difference between Janine and other FS experts, however, is her intuition. She doesn't just use FS. She uses a variety of metaphysical and intuitive tools to provide the best solution to a particular problem. You'll love getting immersed in this work with Janine as your guide.

Katya Varbanova, Entrepreneur and Public figure at Katya.com

T0284385

Even though I have studied Feng Shui it's been a while since I was active in that 'world'. Reading *Feng Shui Your Way to Abundance* renewed my enthusiasm for Feng Shui and the results which you can achieve by applying its principles. *Abundance* works brilliantly on so many levels—beginners can easily understand and action the information provided, people with some knowledge can make use of the handy charts and extend their learning, and the more advanced Feng Shui enthusiasts have all the information they need at their fingertips, alongside extra, non-Feng Shui hints and tips which can be used in conjunction with their existing knowledge. Janine's inspirational examples of Feng Shui in action show that she 'practises what she preaches'. *Abundance* reflects Janine's sense of humour and leaves you with a great feeling of optimism that you can make changes for the better in your life by using the easy to follow techniques described in the book and without spending a fortune.
Lynette McDonald-Cheesman, Company Director

Janine makes a Feng Shui visit to our home each year. We value her knowledge, insight and advice. I really enjoyed using her first book, *Manifest Journal,* and can't wait to see what new Feng Shui advice her second book has to offer.
Jill Lance, Client

Janine's book really gets under your skin in the best possible way. You'll find yourself mindlessly tweaking your space piece by piece as time goes on, and you understand that it's the knowledge of how to optimize your space sinking in. My Feng Shui coins are a permanent fixture now at my front door.
Kellie Blondel, Lead Implementer & Decision Maker @ Virtual Collaborative

Feng Shui Your Way to Abundance

Feng Shui Your Way to Abundance

Janine Lowe

BOOKS

London, UK
Washington, DC, USA

CollectiveInk

First published by O-Books, 2024
O-Books is an imprint of Collective Ink Ltd.,
Unit 11, Shepperton House, 89 Shepperton Road, London, N1 3DF
office@collectiveinkbooks.com
www.collectiveinkbooks.com
www.o-books.com

For distributor details and how to order please visit the 'Ordering' section on our website.

A CIP catalogue record for this book is available from the British Library.

Design: Lapiz Digital Services

UK: Printed and bound by CPI Group (UK) Ltd, Croydon, CR0 4YY
Printed in North America by CPI GPS partners

The author of this book does not dispense medical advice or prescribe the use of any technique as a form of treatment for physical, emotional, or medical problems without the advice of a physician, either directly or indirectly. The intent of the author is only to offer information of a general nature to help you in your quest for emotional and spiritual well-being. In the event you use any of the information in this book for yourself, which is your constitutional right, the author and the publisher assume no responsibility for your actions.

We operate a distinctive and ethical publishing philosophy in all areas of our business, from our global network of authors to production and worldwide distribution.

Contents

Introduction   1

Chapter One: Abundance   9

Chapter Two: Basic Concepts of Feng Shui and
             How to Use Them   14

   Bagua (Energy) Map   14

   Lo Shu Grid   20

Chapter Three: Bagua Map & Nine Life Areas   23

Chapter Four: Feng Shui Your Garden   44

Chapter Five: Flying Stars   56

Chapter Six: Useful Feng Shui Tools   71

Chapter Seven: Common Mistakes   87

Chapter Eight: Chinese Astrology and Feng Shui   94

Chapter Nine: Your Birth Element and
             How to Use It   106

Chapter Ten: Mindset and Manifestation   116

Chapter Eleven: Feng Shui in Action   132

Conclusion   143

Flying Stars Cheat Sheet   145

Also by This Author

Manifest Journal for Inspirational People
ISBN 979-871061-356-6

Date, Love, Marry, Avoid: Find Your Soulmate
ISBN 978-1-80341-376-1

Feng Shui Your Way to Abundance

By Feng Shui Consultant

Janine Lowe

Feng Shui Your Way to Abundance
By Janine Lowe
Award Winning UK Feng Shui Consultant

Introduction

I wrote *Feng Shui Your Way to Abundance* because I wanted to share my knowledge and experience using Feng Shui over the past 16 years to help people create the lives they really want. Seeing the happiness and satisfaction that achieving this has brought into their lives has made me want to share it with more people than I can reach in my one-to-one sessions.

Over the years, most of my clients have told me that the one thing they really desire is more abundance. That's the reason I decided to concentrate on creating abundance using this book. Abundance means different things to all of us. Whether it means more time with your loved ones, greater knowledge, wealth, or good fortune, we all want more of it and this book is going to show you how to achieve your goals.

We live in a time when the message of scarcity seems to be the way of the world. We are constantly told there is not enough for all of us. But that simply isn't true. There is. You just need to understand how to use energy to activate the right areas to bring about the life changes you really want.

This book will show you how to use Feng Shui to attract positive energy to bring those changes into your life. It will help you if your life isn't what you'd like it to be right now. It will show you how to use the energy of your home and your personal energy to attract exactly what you want into your life. You'll benefit from the work I've done over the past 15 years with clients, showing them how to use energy constructively to activate the areas in their homes and offices to bring greater abundance to them.

I practise what I preach. I've used these strategies and tools for myself in my own homes, offices, and gardens. Thanks to Feng Shui, I get to travel all over the world to consult with my clients.

My passion lies with Feng Shui and helping people. My love of buildings adds an extra dimension to what I do. I have a knack for getting the best out of a space, depending on what area my client is looking to activate. Buildings have living, flowing (or stagnant) energy. I can tap into it, using my knowledge and experience to get them exactly what they want.

This is the book I would've liked to find when I was first interested in Feng Shui. I wanted something to explain the basic principles and offer me the right tools and expert knowledge to use in my home, office, and garden. That's what I've pulled together here for you.

You'll learn the principles of Feng Shui and how they are applied to the nine areas of your home, office, and garden. I've made the information and advice in this book accessible so that you can use it to positively influence the energy around you.

This book will change your life. You will be in control of the changes every step of the way. You will learn how to use energy to ensure it flows, and activate those areas that might be stagnant right now.

Let's talk about Feng Shui and what it's all about. Technically Feng means wind (energy), and Shui means water (which gives flow to energy). I can understand why that might sound confusing, but it's simple. We are all affected by energy. We know wind and water are energies that create movement. Our homes are no different. Using Feng Shui is one significant way to activate the important areas you choose to change in your life.

For thousands of years, the Chinese have been aware of how our environments affect our inner and outer lives, including our abundance, relationships, and sense of well-being. They use Feng Shui (pronounced Feng Shway) to enhance their inner lives and their outer signs of success.

They are not the only ones. The Japanese refer to it as Fu-Sui and have also used it for many years. In Hong Kong, they use it when they build commercial buildings to ensure they make more money than their competitors.

You don't need to understand this to benefit from this book, but Feng Shui is rooted in Taoism (pronounced Daoism). The definition of Taoism below will help you see the connection to what we discuss in this book.

> *Taoism [is] the way of man's cooperation with the course or trend of the natural world, whose principles we discover in the flow patterns of water, gas, and fire, which are subsequently memorialised or sculptured in those of stone and wood, and, later, in many forms of human art.*
>
> (*From* Tao: The Watercourse Way, *Alan Watts, 11 July 2019*)

These practices have been used for centuries to aid people to live well. And I am sure they will continue to be used for many years after we are no longer here.

In simple terms, Feng Shui is about arranging our homes, offices, or gardens to achieve harmony with our environment. This enables us to live our best lives. I'll show you how to use objects, space, and directions to activate and improve the areas of your life that matter most to you.

At some level, you will be aware of the energy of spaces in your home and how they affect you. Do you have a favourite part of your home? Do you have a space where you feel relaxed and calm? Or is there a spot where you feel more motivated and get loads done? Are there parts of your house where you feel frustrated or tired? At a subconscious level, you already feel these differing energies.

There are a lot of books about Feng Shui out there. I'm writing this one because I wanted to bring together everything I would've liked to know all those years ago.

So, what can I offer and what should you expect from this book?

- The 'why' Feng Shui works and the 'how'. So many books in this area fail to show people 'how' to use it effectively.
- If other books do cover the 'how', they are often so densely packed with information and terms that readers can't get their heads around it. This book will be easy to understand and put into practice.
- I utilise my extensive experience using Feng Shui for myself and my clients to show you how it can make a huge difference in your life.
- On top of the practical tools for creating positive change in your homes, I use the power of manifestation. I've included it here as another invaluable tool to exponentially increase the powerful energy bringing you your best life.
- I've added a chapter with client stories to demonstrate how I've used Feng Shui to enhance their lives. You will be able to see how I've used it with real people, just like you.
- This book is easy-to-follow and straightforward to action. It's packed with tools that anyone can use.

Before we move on to Chapter One, where I cover the basics of Feng Shui, I have some tips for you to get the most out of this book.

First, I recommend you don't try to change everything at the same time. Simple, sustainable changes will last longer. I advise people to pick three areas of their life they'd most like to improve significantly.

There's a good chance that you're already happy with how some of these areas in your life are going. This process works best if you focus on the areas you'd most like to change. If your love life is great, then you don't need to activate that area. If your career is on track, that might not be one of your choices. If paying your mortgage or bills feels difficult, then wealth may be one area you want to focus on. If you want to improve your family relationships, that could be another. Studying might be something you've always wanted to do; that could be the third area.

Even taking the time to consider what is not working as well as what you'd like in your life will give you a deeper understanding of your priorities.

Don't try to take on all three areas at once. Pick the most important to you and focus on that. Once you've made the changes you need to activate the energy in that area, the results will motivate you to start on the next. I've seen clients try to take on all three at once and become overwhelmed. The usual outcome is that they give up and don't get the results they want.

I have included manifestation because it has a special magic all of its own. If you've used it, you already know that to be true. If you use the tools in this book alongside manifestation, you will create positive change and supercharge your life in the areas you choose to activate.

You can cherry-pick which chapters and tools to follow by choosing those that are most interesting to you, but it will help you to read it all, so you know which parts you'd like to go back to. You will find that I've repeated some of the information throughout the book, in particular references to the nine life areas. I've done this so that you don't have to keep going back and forth in the book to remind yourself what they are. So, any repetition is designed to avoid you having to jump between chapters to check details.

This isn't just any Feng Shui book. Alongside my Feng Shui consulting, I am a Chinese Astrology practitioner. I have found they work together incredibly well to help my clients create the lives they really want. For that reason, I have included information on Chinese Astrology and some of the crossover between the two. You get the benefit of both in this book. If you're not sure which animal you are in Chinese Astrology (this is the Chinese equivalent of Western signs of the Zodiac), don't worry as I'll explain how to work it out in Chapter Seven.

If you're concerned that you won't get the benefits of Feng Shui if you don't believe in it, then let me put your mind at rest. If you follow the actions I've outlined in this book, you will get the results you want.

In fact, I can give you an example of the results achieved by just one of the people I've worked with who didn't believe in it at all. I had a client whose parents were trying to sell their home. It had been on the market for nine months with no success. I advised her to tell her parents to remove a freezer from their home. Even though they didn't believe the advice for a minute, they removed the freezer. The same afternoon that they followed my advice, they got an offer on the house. Now they believe!

If you're concerned that it won't help you, even though it's helped my clients and myself, know that if you follow the tools I outline in this book — it will help you!

In Chapter One, we're going to talk about abundance. In Chapter Two, I'll introduce you to the basics of Feng Shui, so you get a sense of it. Then I will show you tools to use in each of the sections of your home to activate the areas you want to improve. This won't make sense to you yet, but each part of your house is related to an area of your life, and that is how we know which space to activate to achieve the benefits you want.

Feng Shui has been helping people for thousands of years. If you use these tools and knowledge, it will help you too.

Chapter One

Abundance

Before we dive into Feng Shui and how to use it, I want to talk about abundance. This book is about using Feng Shui and the positive energy in your home to attract the abundant life you want. Before we move forward, we need to discuss what it is and what it means to you.

What Is Abundance?

Abundance means a large quantity of something important to us. Most of us seek an abundant life, but it means different things to all of us.

For some, it's about having more time to spend with family and friends. For others, it's about experiences, travel, and knowledge. Many of us think of it in terms of prosperity — which can mean thriving and being successful financially, spiritually, emotionally, or in terms of well-being. Many consider it to be about wealth, financial assets, and material possessions.

A straightforward way to think about it is having plenty of what you most desire, whether that's experiences, contentment, money, or something else entirely.

My clients have identified a whole range of things that represents an abundant life to them; these are just some:

- A happy life
- A loving partner
- Friends who have their back
- Wealth
- Good health
- A roof over their head
- A furry family to share their life with

- Opportunities in their career
- Chances for a different life than they'd grown up with
- Learning how to enjoy the small things in life
- Knowing that tomorrow is going to be okay
- Experiences, adventures, and travel

For this book to work, take some time to consider what it means for you. Don't think about it in terms of what other people want you to have or to be; it's about what YOU value and want more of in your life. Achieving an abundant life only works if it's about what you want.

To know if we've succeeded, we need to define what success looks like.

Is it money you're seeking to have in abundance? Is it about having choices to do what you want for the rest of your life? Is it a loving relationship? Is it about finding a career you're passionate about rather than one you should go into?

Before you read further, decide what abundance looks and feels like to you. Then you will know what it looks and feels like when you've achieved it.

Motivation

Now you've decided what abundance is to you, ask yourself why you want it. We all want more of what we genuinely value and don't feel we have enough of. What is your motivation? What is driving this change? Do you want it badly enough to make changes and take action?

In my experience, people want abundance because it gives them security and stability. They don't have to worry about how they will pay their bills if they have enough money. It can give them the freedom to choose how they want their lives to look and feel. It can allow them to make clear and confident decisions. You will have heard the term 'abundance mindset'. While we talk about mindset later in this book, it refers to people who attract abundance easily into their lives by choosing not to use a scarcity mindset, using what they have correctly, and showing gratitude for what they have received.

Whether you define abundance as being financially comfortable, having the support of a loving family or partner, or having the opportunity to be more creative in your life, the question is, why do you want it?

What is motivating you to create abundance in your life? Do you want it badly enough to take action to achieve it? Understanding your motivation will help you get the most out of this book.

Language

Words have power. The language we use to express what we want has power. The language we use is critical to achieving what we want. Let's talk about the words you use when you talk about what you want.

Using positive and empowering language helps the universe to hear what you are asking for. Don't use qualifying words like 'could' or 'should'. State clearly and positively, 'I accept the abundance of the perfect opportunities you are providing me with to have the career I dream of.' Or, 'I accept gratefully the abundance of wealth you provide me to travel the world and have exciting new adventures.'

Gratitude is a potent tool. The language we use around it can attract the abundance we want. Telling the universe we are grateful and appreciate the positive and wonderful things in our lives helps us keep a perspective about what we already have, and goes on to attract more of the same. If we are going to attract more of what we put out to the universe, then we want to make sure it's the good stuff.

The language we use when we're speaking to ourselves is critical. We must believe and send positive messages about ourselves to the universe. Consistent and regular self-belief is one of the most powerful things we can have to attract abundance.

We're quick to see our flaws but much slower to see our unique qualities and skills. It helps to write down what you bring to the world so you can capture and express it on paper. Do the same for others; there's more than enough abundance to go around. Seeing the good in others has the same effect as expressing gratitude; it attracts more positive energy and abundance back to you.

Despite our best efforts, we all have setbacks. Don't throw in the towel. Once you're through the immediate fallout, think about what happened and any positives which have resulted from the situation. It might be as simple as learning from our mistakes. We learn so much more from failures than from successes. There is almost always something positive we can take from an experience, even if it's as simple as seeing how resilient we are in a crisis.

Try to spend time in your circle of family, friends, and work colleagues (where possible). Choose to be with optimistic people who give off positive energy. Work to surround yourself with positivity, gratitude, and optimism. It will help you build your reserves of positive energy. It won't help to spend time with doubting Debbies or negative Nigels. Everyone has bad days, but if there are people who constantly drain your good vibe, choose some other folk to spend time with.

The thought processes behind attracting abundance are impacted by using positive language, including manifestation, visualisation, and taking action. Using these processes daily means the universe hears what we are saying, thinking, and the energy we put into the world. If you're projecting negativity, a lack of self-belief, or a scarcity mindset, that's what the universe will act upon. I discuss this in more detail in Chapter Ten.

Before you read further, remember to think about what abundance means to you. Be bold and brave, and imagine what your ideal life will look and feel like.

In the next chapter, I will explain the basics of Feng Shui.

Chapter Two

Basic Concepts of Feng Shui and How to Use Them

In this chapter, I'm going to introduce you to some of the key concepts of Feng Shui. Knowing these will help you understand how you can activate the energy in your home to attain the life you want.

Bagua (Energy) Map

The first place to start is with a Bagua Map. It's one of the primary tools we use in Feng Shui. In simple terms, it maps the main areas that affect our lives. Each of the areas on the map relates to a part of our life, including relationships, careers, well-being, and knowledge, to name just a few.

There are nine of these areas, and, aside from the Centre, they each relate to a direction—South, South-East, North, North-East—you get the picture. Completing a Bagua Map is the first thing you should do when you're getting ready to activate the positive energy in your home.

Completing a Bagua Map

You may have heard you can do this using your front door. I personally do not recommend this approach. Using the front door to determine your home's directions means you won't be able to identify the exact directions for your map. What appears to be 'North' in relation to your front door isn't necessarily where North really is. Using the Centre of the house means that you can locate the correct directions in your home and maximise the energy flow in your house. Doors, however, are auspicious. I will cover why they are so important later in the book.

Finding the Centre of Your Home

If you've got a floor plan for your house, this is straightforward. Draw a line across the width of your home and another across the length of your house. The point they intersect is the Centre of your home.

See the diagram below. Of course, most of us don't have perfectly square homes, but you'll get the idea.

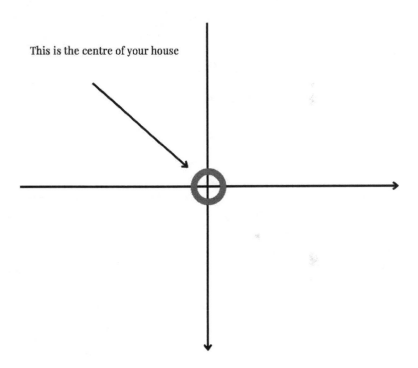

This is the centre of your house

If you haven't got a floorplan for your home—don't worry. You only need to walk from one side of your house to the other to measure the width. Let's use the example in the diagram below, where the house is 16 steps wide. Walk from the front of your home to the back to measure the length. In the diagram below, the length is 20 steps.

Divide the width in half, which is eight steps. Walk eight steps into your house and mark that spot with a cup, bowl, or something small you won't trip over.

Divide the length of your house in half, which is ten steps. Walk ten steps into your home. The point where both meet is the Centre of your house. Happily, there is only one spot where the eighth step from the side and tenth step from the front of your home will meet.

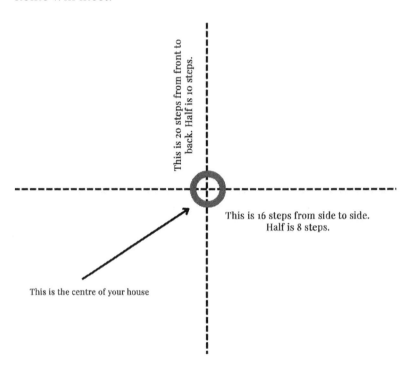

This is 20 steps from front to back. Half is 10 steps.

This is 16 steps from side to side. Half is 8 steps.

This is the centre of your house

It is that simple.

Different House Shapes

If your house isn't square or equal on each side, you need to know which parts to count as part of your home and which not to.

Many houses aren't perfectly square. Some homes are built around a courtyard or form an L-shape. My advice is the same. Measure the width of the widest part of the house and the length of the longest part. Find the midpoint of each. Then locate where the middle of the length and the midpoint of the width intersect. That will be the Centre of your house.

The main aim is to find the Centre of your house so that we can locate the directions for the Lo Shu Grid. We can't apply Feng Shui until we do that.

Flats and Apartments

If you have a flat, it's not the Centre of the building you're looking for; it's the Centre of your flat. You only count your own property, not other people's, in working out where the Centre is.

Garages

Do you include an integral garage? The answer is yes—you need to include the garage when finding the Centre of your home. You must include those because so many use them to store rubbish. It's part of your house, and if it has junk, it must be considered to effectively Feng Shui your home. You need to clear it, tidy it, and declutter it in the same way you do other areas of your home so that it doesn't affect whichever part of your life falls into that part of the grid.

Conservatories, Extensions, and Balconies

If you have a very small part of your house that falls outside the rest of your home, then you don't include it. See the example below for clarity on whether to include these extra sections.

If your house has a very small extension like a conservatory or bay window, don't include it in your Bagua Square.

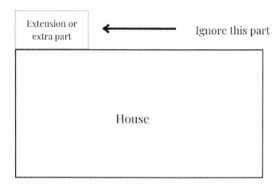

If it forms a significant part or percentage of your house, then include it and square off the missing piece as if it forms part of your home. See the example below.

If your house has a large part outside of the 'square' of your house then square off your home.

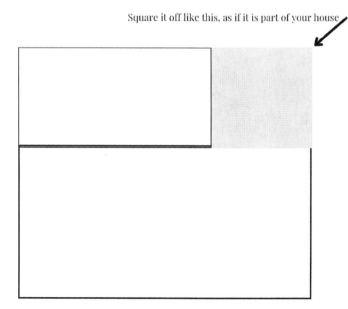

There are very straightforward ways to make that space form part of your home and ensure that energy flows there. I go into more detail on that later in the book.

I have an Art Deco home; the part missing in my house is 'Good Fortune'. For that reason, I've put a pond in so that there is always activity in that area. It doesn't have to be a pond. It can be a water feature of some kind. You don't want a lack of activity in any area of your house, particularly if it's one of the three areas you've chosen to activate.

That brings us to the next step in applying the Lo Shu Grid to our houses. How do I know which part of my home is 'Good Fortune'? Let me explain.

Bagua Map Areas

First, go back to the Centre of your home. Stand there, and from that point, you will be able to locate the following directions:

North
North-East
East
South-East
South
South-West
West
North-West

Phone apps can find these directions if you don't have a compass. Do this standing in the Centre of your room. It's best if you don't wear any jewellery when you do it, as metal can cause a false reading.

These are the degrees of each direction you're looking for once you've found North.

North – 0 degrees
North-East – 45 degrees
East – 90 degrees
South-East – 135 degrees
South – 180 degrees
South-West – 225 degrees
West – 270 degrees
North-West – 315 degrees

These degrees are always the same. They are not impacted by what year we are in. However, some parts of Feng Shui are affected annually, like Flying Stars. We will discuss those in Chapter Five.

Lo Shu Grid

Each of these directions correlates to an area of our lives. When you want to manifest positive change in specific areas of your life, these are the parts to focus on. Check out the grid image on the next page. Then I'll explain what each of these areas relates to.

As you can see from the Lo Shu Grid, the areas are as follows:

Centre – this area is about well-being and is not an area I would activate as it should be kept quiet, clear, and calm.
North – a critical area in Feng Shui relating specifically to career, new beginnings, and spirituality.
North-East – all about wealth and knowledge.
East – this space is about ancestry and romance.
South-East – relates to good fortune and whatever that means to you. It means different things to everyone.
South – this area is about fame and illumination. It's also the area I refer to as 'Nooky time'. Don't put your bed in this area if you want to sleep.

South-West – this space is about you and your partner only. You don't want anything about your children or others in this area.

West – creativity and children are what this area is all about. It's an area to activate if you want to have children or even 'birth' a book or painting.

North-West – if you're trying to attract helpful people or travel and adventure, this is the area for that.

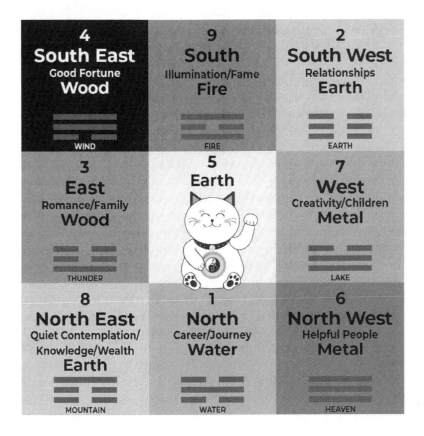

4 South East Good Fortune Wood	9 South Illumination/Fame Fire	2 South West Relationships Earth
WIND	FIRE	EARTH
3 East Romance/Family Wood	5 Earth	7 West Creativity/Children Metal
THUNDER		LAKE
8 North East Quiet Contemplation/ Knowledge/Wealth Earth	1 North Career/Journey Water	6 North West Helpful People Metal
MOUNTAIN	WATER	HEAVEN

As you can see from the Lo Shu Grid above, each area has a number attached to it. These are known as 'the statutory' numbers, and those numbers don't change. This will make more sense to you when you read Chapter Five on Flying Stars. The elements related to each of the areas can also be found in the grid (the Trigrams placed at the bottom of the areas have their own names, some of which share the same name as the element).

In the next chapter, we will dig deep into the Bagua Map and what the areas above are all about.

Chapter Three

Bagua Map & Nine Life Areas

Bagua Map Areas

In the last chapter, I told you how to find the centre of your home and use that to locate the eight other areas of the Bagua Map. Here I'm going to tell you more about the nine areas of our homes and what they represent in Feng Shui.

North

The North is all about careers, endings, and new beginnings. When this area is activated properly, it can change people's lives. Imagine 'when one door closes, another opens' in practice. However, it should only be used in auspicious years which are calculated based on your Chinese animal and Flying Stars. Don't worry if that doesn't make sense yet; it will when you get to the Flying Stars in Chapter Five and Chinese Astrology in Chapter Eight.

The best way to get good sleep is by laying with the top of your head facing North. This is particularly significant if you're struggling with insomnia, which is surprisingly common. This is an easy fix. We refer to laying with the tops of our heads facing north as 'the sleep of the dead'.

The element for the North is water. If you want to activate this area to advance your career, you can do that with water features. A metal water feature is even better because metal enhances the positive water element. Inside you can use a fish tank. If the water is moving, it doesn't need fish in it. The movement of water activates positive Chi or energy. You need a sizeable amount of water to activate energy — so don't just use a cup full.

You can put up pictures or paintings here that represent water but be thoughtful about it. You wouldn't want an image of a shipwreck because that represents chaos. Unless drama and upheaval are what you're looking for in your career, then choose a gentle seascape or a waterfall. You have to use water for activation, but images help reinforce the intention of your goal.

I help my clients further by using their birthdates to determine which dates are auspicious for them to activate the energy in this area and place water features. If you'd like me to do this for you, you can find me at: https://www.janinelowe. co.uk/

Clutter will dampen or stagnate the energy in this space. If you have clutter here, your career will stand still. If you want to place plants here, only have a few because they will bring too much earth energy. If you put in a lot of earth energy, it will stagnate the water energy of the area. It is best to avoid placing your cooker here, but it's fine for your freezer, fridge, or washing machine.

The North is one of the most critical parts of the house because it's one of the most auspicious/favourable areas. I usually activate this area for clients unless it is a year when the 5 Earth Star is visiting the North in the year it needs to be kept calm and quiet. I will tell you about the 5 Earth Star in the Flying Stars chapter.

This is an example of my helping a client activate the North of their home. My client's wife called me to help him. He was very unhappy. He felt he was working all week, having to do jobs around the house on weekends, and didn't have time for himself. His wife worried that his job was taking over his life, and there seemed to be no time for fishing, which was his favourite hobby. She'd started to feel like she was nagging him. He said he felt no one was looking out for him at the office.

His boss didn't appreciate him, and he was struggling to force himself to go to work.

I started in the North and discovered a dripping tap. Taps are good in this area, but not if they're not functioning properly. There was a lot of junk and bric-a-brac in the garden outside. It was a completely unloved and unused area. The garden led into the conservatory, which was full of toys the kids no longer played with. They'd just ignored that part of their house and garden. It was an easy consultation because I knew he wanted a new job. He wanted to enjoy his life more and spend happier times with his family.

I spent time with him and his wife to find out what parts of his life were not working for him anymore. I discovered he wanted to work fewer hours and earn more money, but he didn't want to do that in his current job. He didn't want a career change, but he did need to shift departments and positions.

I helped him put what he wanted on a manifestation board so he could focus and reflect on it. He put it up in the conservatory. Plumbers came in and fixed the dripping tap. They cleaned out the conservatory, and he even started using that space to work.

I wanted to continue to activate this area, so I used the garden. I found the precise North in the garden and used a water feature. We didn't use a pond because they wanted immediate change. We used an electric-powered water feature in the North of the garden. I don't use solar-powered water features because the water must move consistently.

When this was finished, the changes came incredibly fast. Another manager in his company saw his work and offered him a job in his department. He ended up with more people working for him, got an increase in wages, and worked fewer hours. He had more time to do things at home, so he could go fishing every Saturday. Sundays they spent together as a family.

In this case, the activation was done at a human, heavenly, and ground level.

Summary
Always keep the North clear and uncluttered, and use moving water to activate this area.

North-East
The North-East is all about wealth and knowledge. It's one of the areas I tend to activate most in clients' houses or offices. More often than not, the North-East corner tends to be an office, snug, or lounge room.

You can use the symbolism of a library here. It's a place to learn. Keep your books and history here. You must not over-clutter in this area. Only keep books that you use or are important to you. This area is also a wealth space, so it's an excellent place to keep your valuables or a safe.

Wealth and knowledge are not something you sleep on; you need to activate them. The element of the North-East is earth, so use a lot of the colour red in soft furnishings. Use earthy and rich reds rather than sexy, eye-popping reds. This area should be cosy and have a feeling of luxury about it.

I painted this area upstairs in my home rich red and matched it with a greyish-brown colour. The same space downstairs is the kitchen, which is perfect because the cooker is there. If your North-East has a kitchen, use utensils and electric equipment in the colour red to symbolise wealth. Red is very auspicious in the Chinese culture. The Chinese word for red sounds like wealth in their native tongue. In auspicious years, you can also activate this area outside with a water feature.

To get the most out of this area, you need to set the intention to spend a lot of time there. Consciously add colour to this space. Another thing that will help get movement is sorting your finances out in that part. It's a perfect place to study. It's a great place for your child to do their homework if they struggle. Keep it a quiet space and avoid anything stopping you from concentrating, like televisions.

The worst thing you can do is let this area get cluttered. It must be somewhere you feel comfortable working and focusing on your studies and finances. I place three Chinese coins in the wealth area at 30 degrees in a red box to set the intention of bringing wealth into my life.

One of the clients I helped to activate this area wanted their son to get into a private school on a scholarship. His chart showed me that he was clever enough, but his mind was too full and busy. He was struggling to settle down to study or do his homework. He spent most of his time playing computer games or with friends. He had become the class clown. I could see that his behaviour stemmed from boredom. He was an A-grade student who wasn't getting A grades.

I recommended placing him in their North-East area to study. I used his chart to determine what times of the day would suit him best to study. He's a Monkey in Chinese Astrology, so his best times to do homework were between 9–11am and 3–5pm. I had to make it clear to his mother that he couldn't be constantly studying, so outside of those hours, he needed time off. No one can concentrate on work or study all of the time.

Her son started to blossom. He enjoyed his study times, and his schoolteachers remarked on the change in him. He got his scholarship for the private school his mother wanted him to go to.

Chinese Astrology can help us to get the best results in our lives. I cover this briefly later in this book. I'm writing this on a Dragon Day. I am a Rooster in Chinese Astrology, and Roosters are special friends of Dragons. To get the best results writing this book, I've chosen to work at the best times for Roosters, which are 07.00–11.00 and 17.00–19.00. Working in these two-hour stints means I also get time to let my brain rest in between.

Using this approach has made writing this book so much easier. Everyone has auspicious hours to work in. I've included those in Chapter Eight on Chinese Astrology.

Let me tell you about another client who called me in to help her child. She was sure he had ADHD. He was super intelligent. Although I'm no expert, it was clear that he didn't have ADHD. From his date of birth, I could see that he was incredibly clever but needed guidance in subjects that interested him.

I helped his mother activate the North-East of their house to help him focus on his study and homework. However, that wasn't the whole problem, and it's normal for me to need to activate more than one area in a consultation. I checked where he was sleeping. The direction the top of his head was facing when he was asleep meant that his brain wasn't getting enough rest. I moved his bed so that the top of his head was facing North. He got more sleep, and it allowed his brain to regenerate longer. I also activated a play area for him in the West of their home to help him let off steam when he wasn't studying and sleeping, and placed his favourite hobbies in this area.

As you can tell I spend a lot of time activating the North-East in my clients' homes. Here's another example of a client who was an angel investor who invested in start-up companies. She'd already invited me to do a consultation on her home. She then brought me into one of their offices to ensure each team member was in the right position within the building to work at their best. Some of the members of her team were not up for it. Not everyone is open to Feng Shui. I didn't mind. I've dealt with sceptics before. Despite their resistance, they followed my advice and moved to the areas I suggested within the building. Some of them even changed roles within the company.

I put the Chief Financial Officer in the North-East, where he was dealing with the start-up's finances. He had his back in the

North-East, which was very auspicious for the company. I had the wall behind him painted red, as this is a supportive colour for wealth in China.

For maximum benefit, I placed the CEO in the North-West as this space represents strong male energy, which supported him in his role. The North-West is also where 'helpful people' are situated in Feng Shui. I was sure that sitting in this area would bring the right people into his office. I arranged for a glass desk. The symbolism of this was to help him make decisions more clearly. His chair was high-backed and sat higher than the chairs of the people in front of him.

I moved the CTO (Chief Technology Officer) to the West of the building. This is the area for creativity. I advised them to paint the room white and grey. One entire wall was whiteboards with a huge TV screen on another wall. The room had hardly any other furniture besides the basics—desk and chairs, alongside his high-tech gear.

I spoke to each of their top directors and anyone else who was up for learning something new. They were young, trendy, and up for trying whatever would work. I identified the best times for each of them to concentrate on work according to their birthdates. If they focused on those hours, they would achieve so much that they could go and chill out during their inauspicious hours. They added a space to allow their team let off steam with pods, a games area, and a snooker table.

I recommended other activations for this company but can't give away their trade secrets. What was the result? The company floated and made its investors a lot of money.

Summary

You need to spend a lot of time intentionally in this space. Decorate it with red and earthy colours; don't forget—no clutter, or you will mess with your finances.

East

The East of our houses is all about romance, past histories, and ancestry within your family. I don't tend to work in this area much with my clients. It doesn't come up as a priority area very often. But if it is for you, then read on.

This is the area I often refer to as the 'dustbin' area. If you want to keep an item because it's important to you but don't know where to put it, keep it in the East. Don't keep things that are useless or broken or anything you feel you 'should' save. If you don't want the table Granny left you, it really is time to get rid of it. Whatever you do keep in there must be kept clean, tidy, and in good working order. Don't let it get cluttered, or you won't be able to see the wood for the trees on any decisions or issues.

The East is great for married couples who want more romance. It can make a great bedroom. Use calm colours when decorating—tranquil pale blues and greens will work well here. Keep your soft furnishings luxurious. If you want to activate this area, make it feel dreamier and a little sexier than you would the couple's area of your house in the South-West.

The element for the East part of our homes is wood, and the element that activates wood is water. So, if you want to activate this area, use a water feature outside or a fish tank inside. It's worth checking the Flying Stars before you do that. Don't use reds in this area of your house, that will add a fire element which won't work with the wood element of the East.

Don't put too much furniture in your East bedroom if you're trying to activate romance. A bed, a couple of side tables, and perhaps even a make-up table are enough. You do not want this space crammed. Likewise, you do not want to use music or technology here.

Some houses have staircases in the East. One great way of activating the energy is to have a gallery of pictures of you and your family, past and present, all the way up the stairs.

Strangely, one area of your life that can be helped by activating the East of your home relates to dealing with legal issues or solicitors. Activate this area with water if you want some positive movement in legal matters. It is also useful to activate this area if you are a solicitor or a person who deals with legal documents.

If you're lucky enough to have a front door in the East, paint it blue to bring in the positive Chi from outside.

I was once called in to help a couple experiencing problems with their teenagers and parents. It was causing them to feel alienated. The first thing that struck me when I arrived was that the house felt utterly barren. Everything was focused on one child who had special needs. The child with the problem was a 17-year-old teenager. Her parents were not aware that she was taking drugs and was attracted to women. She was worried that they wouldn't accept her as she was. I spent a lot of time talking to her and suggested she tell them what she'd told me.

I advised the parents to fill their East wall with photos of their happy childhoods with their parents, their children with their grandparents, and themselves with their children. I wanted them to focus on happy times and memories with each other. I recommended that all of the generations participate in putting the wall together. They were invited to come over and talk about it over shared meals. The photos needed to be in matching wooden frames to activate the area. Whether they were vertical, horizontal, square, or rectangular didn't matter. The shared project made a huge difference in all of their relationships.

The teenager told her parents what she had been keeping to herself. They weren't surprised at all. They let her grow and bloom in her own way.

Another example of where I activated the East of a home happened when a couple came to me because they were constantly arguing. I could see that the East bedroom was their problem. If the East is not looked after, it can cause anger and family quarrels. It can also cause illness. I suggested they decorate the room together, choosing colours, furniture, and soft furnishings in tranquil, dreamy colours. I moved their bed so that the tops of their heads were both facing East to enhance the romance in their lives again.

I recommended they spend time together in this room. Their new, shared bedroom brought about a new romantic relationship. They became so much happier and stopped arguing as much.

Plans to alter and activate the East area of homes can take time to put in place, but the results are quick.

In both cases, I advised the families involved to activate the East of their homes by putting their water features outside. The Chi was incredibly negative in both cases, so it felt important to bring in the positive Chi from outside and release the negative Chi.

Summary

Activate this area with water. Choose dreamy, tranquil colours and luxury textures to bring more romance into your lives. If you have items you don't feel fit anywhere else in your home, this area could be where they are placed, as long as they aren't broken, and you use them now or in the future. Make sure it's not cluttered, and keep it clean and tidy.

South-East

The South-East is all about good fortune; an auspicious area for everyone. Chinese people love this area in their homes and often set up an altar here to place their intentions and share their gratitude using fresh flowers, statues, and family photos.

This is one of my favourite areas to work on in the Lo Shu Grid. The element is wood. So, we use water to activate it. You can instal a pond if you decide to activate it outside. Inside you can use an aquarium. The more water—the bigger the aquarium, pond, or swimming pool—the more money and good fortune you will attract. Fish are very auspicious in China and can attract exceptional good fortune—so make sure you put them in your ponds and aquariums. I don't recommend having fish in your swimming pool, though. That would just be weird.

Good fortune is not always about money. It can be anything that can make you happy, a new opportunity, a job change, new colleagues, a chance to study or travel, or a house move. Good fortune looks and feels different to everyone. It's whatever it means to you that matters.

One thing you mustn't do is use metal in the South-East of your home, or you may find, if presented with two choices, that you choose the wrong one. If there is too much fire in the area, it will drain the positive energy.

If you don't have a window in the South-East corner of your house, consider placing a clock there for movement. I have a clock in that area of my house. What type of clock is best? One that works and is made of wood; the bigger, the better.

If you're lucky enough to have a door in this area of your house, paint it blue or green.

I was called in to consult with a man who lived by himself. I hadn't looked up where he lived. I never do that. I just put the address in the satnav and let it guide me there.

I arrived at a set of electric gates with a sweeping drive and a huge house behind it. He had a garage full of cars. His home didn't need decluttering. It was a man pad, so it was very minimalistic. It took me hours to get around to each part of the house because it was so big.

He was wealthy, and his wealth area was good, but he wanted more. Given there wasn't much more he needed to do in the wealth area, I worked on his good fortune in the South-East corner of his house. I told him that he needed to place a pond on the outside of the area. He decided to put in a swimming pool instead. I advised him on auspicious days to have it dug out and that it must be open to the air and well-maintained. The pool he put in was huge. He made loads of money, but that wasn't all the good fortune he attracted. I can't share with you what the other good fortune was. Let's just say he was a very happy client.

Summary

None of us can ever have too much good fortune, whatever that means to us. Use water features in this area.

South

The South of our homes is all about fame and illumination. This is particularly important if you want to be an actor, singer, author, or famous for anything.

For me, illumination is about understanding and being true to yourself. Understanding what you want to achieve and tapping into yourself can help you make the most of this area and gain fame. I find it difficult to meditate, but I try to keep my mind still. I am always on the go, so sitting down, I get the proverbial 'ants in my pants'. I have always wanted to write a book. Whilst tuning into myself one week, I realised the way forward for me to write this book was to record it and get my Virtual Assistant to type it up.

Illumination is about knowing clearly what you want and how you need to do it.

The element for the South of our homes is fire. Bright colours are perfect for this area: reds, oranges, yellows, and even some browns and greens. Don't use blue or your intentions will fizzle out. You can use red and green candles here when setting your intentions or manifesting, as the South is where you can meditate and dream about what you want to come true. This space is helpful as somewhere you can stop and think about your life and what you want, so a big sturdy wooden chair covered in red material would be fab here. Perhaps even make a manifestation board. I tell you how to do that in Chapter Ten.

In the South of my home, I have a huge picture of the Brad Pitt movie *Fight Club*, which represents fame and illumination for me. If you use an image, it needs to be vibrant to be effective in this area. By the way, it isn't a picture of him fighting. That would bring a different type of energy in.

Do not use water here and keep the space uncluttered. Both will dampen the energy. Even pictures with water in them aren't great in this area. Definitely do not put a picture of a shipwreck up in the South of your home or office. That will create chaos. You can use pictures of flowers like poppies, roses, or other vibrant options.

If you're lucky enough to have a kitchen in this part of your home, make sure your cooker is placed at 180 degrees; that will generate positive energy.

This is not a quiet area of your home, so it's not ideal for a bedroom. If you're looking for quiet contemplation, use the North of your house for that. The South is an amazing and powerful space but very much an awake area. It works well as an exercise zone, so your exercise bike can go in here. The Horse in Chinese Astrology lives in this area, and Horses are all about passion and new ideas.

Don't ever hand this space over to someone else. If you want to activate your fame or illumination, you need to be in this area to ensure your intentions come to life.

I once consulted with a famous client whose greatest wish was to go on *Strictly Come Dancing*. He was not well known for dancing, but this had been something he'd wanted for a long time. The first thing I did was to check out the South of his house. It was completely barren and empty. Not a lot was happening in there.

He used the South as his lounge room. I added a vibrant red wall and put in a dramatic, huge mirror where he could see himself reflected. I wanted him to visualise himself dancing as he looked at it. The intention was significant; he seriously wanted it. I got him dancing while looking in the mirror to various types of music, even his own songs, as I was sure that when he got on *Strictly Come Dancing*, they would expect him to dance to one of them.

In the South of his garden, we put a sharp Mother Tongue plant with red plants around it. I told him the auspicious days and times to plant it for the best results.

It's important to remember that activating the South is all about setting your intentions clearly and then taking action.

The other area I focused on for him was the North-West, so he would attract well-placed people to come forward to help him realise his dream. He needed them to influence the *Strictly* invitation and some of the dancers he wanted to be his partner.

We started this process at the beginning of April, and he got his offer to go on *Strictly* about a month later. Although he didn't win, he loved it and gained popularity on the show.

Summary

If this is an area you want to activate, do not use water. Use fire and earthy colours—reds, greens, and browns to activate this area with wood and fire elements. For example, use red and green candles and light them with your intentions in mind.

South-West

The South-West is all about relationships. I love working in this area to unite people, especially if they are looking for a life partner. This area on the Lo Shu Grid is where the mother or wife of the home resides. I use it to help support her and bring her dreams to fruition.

Using red and yellow colour soft furnishings brings this area to life. Use beautiful fragrances and scents to set the scene for love. Reds and yellows are great, and you can add pink. If this is a dining area, only put two chairs in place.

Place everything in this area in pairs. One suggestion is to decorate it with pairs of swans (they are auspicious as they mate for life), and pictures of you and your loved one. Make sure they represent happy memories of the two of you together. If you do not have a partner use pictures that symbolise the type of person you are looking for.

Put a peony on the windowsill for love. It is one of the Chinese love flowers. They say your true love may pass your window, see the flower, and come in. I love that idea.

Avoid clutter, or the area will stagnate, which means there won't be any passion or romance. Avoid metal, or it will dampen your mood and affect any positive activation in your relationship area.

You can also use the South-West in your garden, with lush greenery and loads of red, pink, and orange blossoms.

Activating this area is easy. It would help if you spent regular time here. Ensure everything is clean, and don't keep anything broken here. Play music. Beware clutter in this area will ruin a relationship. If it is messy, you must declutter, organise, and tidy, especially if you want a new relationship or to improve your current one.

One client I was called in to consult with had lost her husband. He had died suddenly, and she was in shock. She didn't want to move on but was only in her 40s and lonely. The downstairs of her home was fine. But upstairs, she had a cupboard that was a complete mess. She still had a load of her late husband's clothes in it. We took his clothes out. She chose some she wanted to keep. I told her she could not leave them in her bedroom as this was the relationship area. We didn't want her husband coming between her and a new partner.

I integrated red into her South-West. I also told her that wearing red knickers and red bras was placing her intention for a new partner. She giggled at this but went out and bought them anyway.

Literally, one week after we sorted out that area, she met a guy she'd gone to school with at a local supermarket. It turned out that he had also lost his wife, so he completely understood her situation. They went for coffee, and the rest is history.

Simple decluttering, using red and moving her husband on with love and light was all it took.

Summary

This area is all about the pairs, pinks, and peonies. Bring the romance in, make it only about the two of you, and a bit of red definitely will not hurt.

West

The West of our homes and offices is all about creativity and children. If I'm working with artists, writers, painters, or people creating products, this is one of the areas I activate. As a creative person myself, my office is in the West. I have a clock in my office and artwork specifically selected to promote my creativity. My daughter-in-law has created an artwork with each Chinese Astrology animal for me, and that is on my wall. The best way to decorate this area is to have items that represent you; in my case, that is a clock and books. I love working in this area. As I've mentioned, I am a Rooster in Chinese Astrology, and the West suits Roosters.

The West also represents fun and partying, a great area to get people together.

The best colours to use in the West are greys, silvers, pinks, and purples. If you want children, some red can be used in this area. Avoid wood colours like brown and green.

The element for the West is metal, so avoid water in this area. Instead of using water, you can activate the energy clocks for movement with technology—computers, mobiles, and all things techy. The other activation that works is music; it brings the vibe up.

Set this area up with books and art to make you feel aligned with your dreams. Play music that inspires you.

Use a manifestation board here to create intention and to help activate this area. Although it's best to avoid wood, you can use it for your desk if you add more metal to balance it.

Clutter can dampen the energy. Negative thinking will stagnate the energy in the West. This area is all about positive intentions and magic. Negative thoughts are worse than clutter here.

I have used this area to help people who wanted desperately to have babies but couldn't. In fact, I have helped seven babies to be born by activating this area. In each case, I used people's birthdates, and determined the auspicious dates and times to procreate. Needless to say, the best place to 'do the deed' is in the West.

One of the clients I consulted with was a couple who had been together for years. They'd gone to university together, dated, bought their first house, and then expected to be able to start a family. Unfortunately, that didn't happen. They called me in to help. They'd been together so long they'd lost some of the passion between them. I helped them spice it up by bringing the right colours into the West of their home. I told them what colours to wear, and let them know the best dates and times according to their birthdates to create a baby. I helped them set their clear intention, and they had a baby.

Timing is so important in the West. I can help people identify the most auspicious dates and times based on their birthdates. Then to get the best results, they use that to activate the area and set clear intentions for their dreams to come true.

39

One of my client couples ended up trying for a baby in their garage, and another in a shed to make sure it happened in the right area of their house. Of course, I helped advise them on making it a pleasant space to make babies with the right colours and candles. Fortunately, most of my clients who need to activate this area have been able to set their intentions and take action inside their homes.

Water plays such an important part in many areas in terms of activation but not in the West. It's all about timing, intention, the right elements and, of course, taking action.

Summary

If you'd like to boost your creativity, use greys, silvers, pinks, and purples. If you want to make babies, add a bit of red. Skip the water here, but you can use metal and all things techy.

North-West

Helpful people are those who turn up at the exact time you need them, and you make that happen in the North-West. I activate this area for myself and my clients when I'm asked to bring helpful people into our lives. Many of us tend not to ask for help when we need it. Activating this area will bring the right people to you. All you need to do is accept their help.

When I work with my clients, I use metal inside the house and water outside to activate this area; you will be surprised who turns up in your life to support you. Once this area is activated, you can meet the right people walking your dog in the park, in a café, or anywhere at any time. It creates a special kind of magic.

The colours are the same as in the West—greys, silvers, pinks, and purples, but avoid blues and skip the water element here as well. You can use big earthy plants with round leaves to nurture the energy of this space. Add metal to this area in the form of symbolic artwork, for example, strong male energy such as a lion, inspirational people, or mountains. Metal statues are also best placed here: an elephant with its trunk up facing the door will bring in good fortune to the North-West.

Just as the South-West is the mother and wife area, the North-West is the father and husband area. The South-West is a yin female energy; the North-West is a yang strong male energy. Activation for this area uses music, mirrors, clocks, and techy stuff. Outside in the garden, use water features.

One of my earliest consultations which involved working in the North-West was with a man who lived alone. He had what he needed. For example, he only had enough cutlery for himself. He wanted to change his life. He wanted to meet people. He was charming but stuck in his ways.

As he particularly wanted female company, on this occasion, I suggested we activate both the South-West female energy and the North-West male energy at the same time, to bring both energies together like a thunderclap and let the magic begin.

I set him tasks to do; decluttering was the most important. For some reason, he had about a hundred carrier bags in a cupboard in his helpful people area, and they were all empty bags, empty life. I advised him to buy kitchen utensils to include six of everything, including six cups, plates, and bowls, all in red, and to visualise people sitting around his table.

I was sure he would laugh at my suggestions, but he took them on board and went shopping. He asked me to come and check on him a month later. Even I was surprised at the difference in him. He was smiling, and he looked completely changed in a positive way.

One of the unexpected results of the changes was that a distant cousin had been in touch and had invited him to New Zealand. He jumped at the chance. On the plane, he sat next to a rather outgoing lady, they exchanged numbers, and the relationship built from there. I do love a positive ending.

Summary

Declutter here and use metal inside and water outside to activate bringing the people you need into your life. The colours are the same as in the West—greys, silvers, pinks, and purples.

Centre

The centre of our houses is about well-being. I do not believe that Feng Shui can help people with health issues. That's not to say that working with different areas of your home can't help and support your well-being; it can. I don't tend to activate this part of my clients' houses when I work with them.

But how can you get the best out of this area of your home? My advice is to keep it clean, tidy, and clutter-free. In so many houses the centre is under the stairs. It's okay to store things under your stairs but ensure they are useful and kept tidy. If you've got old, unused paint pots or broken furniture, don't leave them there—get rid of them.

Keep the centre of your house obstacle free. It doesn't matter how pretty that little table is; if it's creating an obstacle to the flow of the centre of your house, don't put it there. This is particularly important in a flat where you have limited space.

Summary

The centre of your home is all about your well-being. Don't activate it; keep it clean, tidy, clutter and obstacle free, and then ignore it.

In Chapter Four, I will tell you how to Feng Shui your garden.

Chapter Four

Feng Shui Your Garden

I don't have green fingers, but I love designing my clients' gardens with Feng Shui to enhance their lives. I really enjoy getting into their gardens to establish what will most attract abundance into their world. Most of the gardens I've consulted on were at clients' homes, but some have been at their business premises. Working on the outside as well as the inside of your home or office is incredibly powerful.

Using the same Feng Shui principles in your garden as we use in your home brings double the Good Fortune and Abundance. It brings a deeper connection with the five elements of Fire, Earth, Metal, Water, and Wood. When they are activated in your garden, they will bring positive energy into your life.

When we work on your house, we bring energy in from the outside. If that's the energy we are bringing into your home, you can imagine the impact of using Feng Shui to enhance the powerful energy in your garden by harnessing the force of nature.

The objective is the same as in your home. Our aim is to create harmonious and balanced positive energy in the nine life areas in your garden. Instead of paintings and candles, we use flowers, trees, ponds, bird baths, garden furniture, statues, and human Chi.

How to Feng Shui Your Garden?

We use the same Lo Shu Grid for your garden as we do in your house. Now that you've read about that, you will know which areas to enhance and which to keep quiet. So that you don't need to flick back to that chapter, I've put the reference points for each area here.

North – Career and New Beginnings 0 degrees
North-East – Wealth & Knowledge 45 degrees
East – Family & Romance 90 degrees
South-East – Good Fortune 135 degrees
South – Fame 180 degrees
South-West – Relationships 225 degrees
West – Creativity 270 degrees
North-West – Helpful People 315 degrees

Just as you did inside your home, stand in the centre of your garden with a compass. If you don't have a compass, you can get apps on your phone. You can also find the centre of your garden by counting the steps from one side to the other, then from front to back, and locate the middle point, where they both meet. If you have a front and back garden, do it for each of them separately.

If you have patios and courtyards rather than a garden, place the Bagua Map on them, even if they're very small. If you have balconies rather than a garden, treat them as part of your house, whichever area they fall into. As I mentioned earlier—small parts can be considered part of your home. You'll remember that you need to stand in the centre of your house and find the exact degree they are on, using the list of degree locations above. You will then know which life area they belong to, and you can enhance that.

Tools for Garden Feng Shui

The advice for your house and garden is the same. The difference lies in the tools and symbols we use to activate and support the areas that are most important to you. Some of my favourite tools to use in gardens are curvy paths, plants, trees, bird baths, ponds, garden furniture, and symbolic statues. I will now run through how you can use each of them in your garden.

Curvy Paths

Why use curvy pathways? A curving path to your front door, or even around your garden, is an effective tool in Feng Shui because it can slow down any fast-moving energy coming into your space. We slow down fast-moving Chi because it can be disruptive, whereas meandering energy is more likely to be harmonious.

When you walk straight to your front or back door, do you stop to take notice of the beautiful plants and flowers in your garden? The chances are that you don't. We're all guilty of this. If you don't notice your journey into your home, it means you are still in work mode. Work mode means you enter your home in what we call Sha Chi. You need to ask yourself if this is the energy you want to flow from your garden into your home. If not, the way around it is to have a curvy path to soften that energy.

If you already have straight paths and it's not practical to change them, place plants or ornaments on them so you have to move around them in a less direct line. Don't put them where you're likely to fall over them in the dark, though. That won't enhance anyone's life.

I use stones and log slabs for the paths around my garden to create the perfect energy for a slower, calmer pace. It's much simpler than having concrete and so much prettier.

When planning your paths, think about the natural contours and curves in your garden. Is there already a flow to your garden that your path could enhance? You may already have plants, shrubs, hedges, or trees forming a natural arc that you can build on and take advantage of.

One simple tool I used when creating my garden was to lay my garden hose in the position where I was planning to place my path. That gave me a chance to visualise what it would look like. It took me a few times to get it right, but the positive energy flow it has created has made it more than worth the time and effort.

Using natural products makes sense. They so often represent the Feng Shui elements. Flagstones, gravel, mulch, and wood for edging and bordering are perfect. I recommend not using solar power for your water features if you're trying to enhance that area. If you want to activate it, the water must always move, whereas solar lighting only works when the sun charges it. If your solar water feature has batteries, you can use them if you keep them constantly charged. While only constantly moving water works for activation, solar lighting can make such a difference to the ambience of your garden, making it pretty and tranquil. It won't enhance energy, but it can make your garden more beautiful.

Once your path is in place, use different colour plants around it that will work with different life areas of your garden. I've added some ideas for plants and trees to enhance the positive energy in those areas.

Trees

Not everyone has a big enough garden for trees, especially those in big cities. But if you are lucky enough to have them, here are some tips on auspicious trees in Feng Shui.

Bamboo is flexible and fast-growing. In Feng Shui, it symbolises strength, endurance, and the ability to go with the flow. It's also associated with good luck and prosperity.

Pine trees are associated with wisdom and can be placed in a garden for protection. Imagine putting that in your garden's knowledge area, particularly if you are studying.

Citrus trees are considered to be good luck, and promote prosperity and abundance. If possible, place them in the South-East of your garden. On the Chinese New Year, celebrating the fruits of these trees symbolises an auspicious year ahead.

Plum trees are highly thought of in Chinese culture for their beauty because they are one of the only trees that bloom in winter and are associated with abundance and good fortune.

Willow trees are great for emotional well-being and bring calming energy. I have a huge willow tree in my garden, and while its size may annoy neighbours, it has brought so much positive energy into my home.

We mustn't forget the Money tree or plant (Pachira aquatica). You can have it inside or outside your home or office, and it's known for attracting wealth and prosperity. The more, the better. You can place more than one in the areas you want to enhance. For the best results attracting wealth, put them in the North-East or South-East.

The Acer, Japanese Maple, Dove tree, Flying Spider Fern, and Golden Larch are other trees that attract good energy.

Inauspicious Trees

Some trees are regarded as inauspicious to have in your garden. Here are a few of those.

Cypress trees have low energy and are thought to attract a depressing attitude.

Dead or dying trees are inauspicious, so remove them as they bring a sense of decay or blockage in the life area they're in. You don't want that in any area of your life, but you definitely don't want it to cause problems for your relationships or wealth.

Thorny trees and plants give off aggressive energy and disrupt the life area they are in. No one wants a career or relationship full of disruption.

Deciduous trees, which lose their leaves every year, shouldn't be placed near the main entrance of your home, office, or garden because that will obstruct the positive energy coming in. In Feng Shui, that represents challenges in your life.

The shape of your tree is important as well. Avoid letting trees grow so much they have overbearing canopies. These are considered to bring heavy energy and block beneficial Chi flow.

Avoid Palm trees because the Chinese call them poison arrows.

Plants

Here are some suggestions for plants to place in the eight areas in your garden to enhance the positive energy flow there. As with your home and office, I haven't suggested plants for the centre of your garden because it's always best to keep that area quiet and uncluttered.

I'm not a gardener, so you must check these plants against the specific soil condition, temperature, and available sunlight where you live before planting them. Every garden is different, and there's no point planting Azaleas if your soil isn't acidic enough. You'll spend a lot of time having to top up your soil with acidic compost. So, keep that in mind when you consider the plants I've mentioned.

South

The best flowers for the South are those that love direct sunlight and potentially hotter temperatures, like Sunflowers, Marigolds, Zinnias, Lantanas, Salvias, Portulacas, Black-Eyed Susans, and Pentas.

South-West

Like the South, this area suits flowers and plants that need full sunlight. Some of the flowers best suited to this area are Roses, Lavender, Salvia, Coneflowers, Cosmos, Gaillardias, Marigold, and Verbena.

West

The flowers and plants for this area are those that need a mix of sun and shade conditions as well as potential exposure to afternoon sun. Some flowers best suited to the West are Geraniums, Coreopsis, Calendula, Daisies, Lobelia, Foxgloves, Hellebores, and Nasturtiums.

North-West

This area is best for those that need a mixture of sun and shade conditions but which also get exposure to cooler temperatures. Some great plants for the North-West are Rhododendrons, Azaleas, Japanese Maples, Ferns, Camellias, Hostas, Witch Hazels, and Bleeding Hearts.

North

Hostas, Astilbes, Bleeding Hearts, Foxgloves, Ferns, Coral Bells, Lungworts, and Jacob's Ladder are the flowers and plants that benefit from being in the North of your garden.

North-East

The North-East can take plants that need both sun and shade and those that grow in cooler temperatures, including Hydrangeas, Astilbes, Columbines, Bleeding Hearts, Primroses, Lungworts, Japanese Anemones, and Hellebores.

East

In the East, you need to put plants that can survive in sun and partial shade, including Daylilies, Irises, Phlox, Coreopsis, Bleeding Hearts, Coral Bells, Balloon Flowers, and Lilies.

South-East

The South-East has both sun and partial shade. Here are some ideas for plants to go there—Gardenias, Daylilies, Hibiscus, Black-Eyed Susans, Coneflowers, Lantanas, Pentas and Verbena.

Fishponds

It's probably already obvious, but I love fishponds. When I moved to my house 21 years ago, I built a fishpond in the centre of my garden. I added nine goldfish, eight oranges and one black fish, because those numbers are said to be most auspicious in Feng Shui. Those fish have multiplied, and there are now 60 of them.

In 2008 I brought in a Feng Shui Master because I wanted to get his take on where he felt the pond should be. As I have an Art Deco house with a missing space in the South-East, he suggested moving the pond there. That was his only recommendation. I moved it and got exactly what I wanted, with a few extra surprises. That's when I knew I wanted to work with water to create and manifest my dream life. Fifteen years later, I'm advising people on how to make that happen for themselves.

I work with water a lot in my clients' houses. I use my Luo Pan, or Feng Shui compass, to find the nine life areas. Generally, I am asked to find the wealth area in their house or business. I always use water for this because it's the perfect activation for wealth and abundance. You can activate once a year at the change of the Chinese New Year or once a month as the Flying Stars move around the house, which is covered in Chapter Five.

Having a fishpond in your garden isn't just good for Feng Shui. There are other benefits. It adds charm and beauty, and visual interest, and can be a focal point. You don't have to have fish in it. Some people love the sound of cascading water, but if you want to attract more abundance, remember nine goldfish, eight orange and one black fish.

Water in a fishpond can have a calming effect in the same way as a gentle water fountain. The movement of the fish in the water can also destress you after a hard day's work. I enjoy watching my fish. I call them, and they all come to the top of the pond. It's probably because they know I'm about to feed them.

On top of that, a well-maintained fishpond can attract a variety of wildlife to your garden, like frogs, birds, dragonflies, and insects, and they can create a diverse and mutually beneficial ecosystem.

Just one tip: shut your windows at night because one of the varieties of wildlife you can attract is mosquitoes, and they can make their presence felt despite their size.

Bird Baths

From a Feng Shui perspective, water features are great to move around yearly according to the Flying Stars residing in whichever area of your garden you want to activate. Bird baths are much easier to move around than other options, like ponds and pools.

The other advantage is that you don't have to worry about the water moving. The birds will do that for you by washing, drinking, and playing around in it, so you won't need any power to keep the water active.

Of course, you're also helping birds to hydrate by keeping the water topped up, particularly in the hot summer months. Just being able to have a water bath keeps dust and parasites off them. Keeping birds clean, safe, and well-hydrated will definitely encourage more positive energy in your garden. Birds are unpaid pest controllers for those garden pests you could do without, the mosquitoes.

Bird baths can be a great centrepiece in your garden, and they're aesthetically pleasing to the eye. Watching birds in them can add to a sense of tranquillity and calm energy.

Here are some tips on installing and looking after your bird bath. They are nothing to do with Feng Shui, but looking after birds and other wildlife adds to the positive energy of our gardens.

Choose a shallow basin or dish with gently sloping sides. If you tend to get larger birds in your bird bath, it may be better to choose a deeper model but remember that smaller birds may drown in deeper water. If your bird bath is deeper, one way to get around this is to put some pebbles or stones in it so that smaller birds can land on these and stay at a safe level above the water.

Keep the bird bath in a safe, quiet place near trees and shrubs so they can escape quickly if any marauding cats are around.

Clean and refill the bird bath regularly to maintain the freshness of the water. This is important from a Feng Shui perspective and also for the health of your local birds. You can only imagine what sort of energy you're activating if your bird bath water is dirty and murky.

One helpful tip is adding a few copper coins to your bird bath water to prevent algae from growing! I'm told that pennies from pre-1982 are better for this because of their metal composition.

Clear the Clutter

You must have known this was coming! Our gardens are no different to our homes or offices in this regard. We must declutter our gardens. It doesn't mean you can't get away with a compost heap—you need one, but that isn't the whole story.

You don't need that broken-down old wheelbarrow your great-aunt Maude gave you or other unused items, like broken pots, garden ornaments, and unused furniture that we all accumulate over time. Trim overgrown plants and remove debris from paths.

Prune and maintain your plants. It will keep them healthy and promote energy growth. Overgrown or diseased plants create a sense of imbalance in the garden next to healthy ones.

Organise your gardening tools. Use proper storage rather than leaving them scattered around the garden. This promotes a sense of order and allows the energy to flow more positively and easily.

Most of us have bins in our gardens—keep them in the East if possible. Don't have your bins near your front door. You do not want inauspicious energy entering the house whenever you open it.

Clear any paths in your garden because this will affect the energy flow. We don't want the negative energy stuck there or to stop positive energy from flowing into the house.

Don't forget to clear your water features and ensure the water is clean and moving, or it can create negative or stagnant energy.

Wind Chimes

Wind chimes create positive energy as long as they don't annoy the neighbours. There's no point in causing a neighbourly dispute. That will not add abundance to your life.

Place them where the breeze can easily catch them. Hang them where they can freely move without hitting walls or trees.

The materials they are made from and the sound they create are important. Find wind chimes made of natural bamboo, glass, and ceramic materials. They come in tinkling noises and deeper tones. Choose one you prefer.

Consider harmonious shapes and colours that will flow in your garden and complement the area you place them in.

Pick your wind chime to complement the features you already have in your garden. Your ponds and bird baths are centrepieces. Your wind chime shouldn't be dominant.

They can't be used to activate areas of your garden. Only water can do that, but they contribute to positive energy.

In Chapter Five, I will tell you about Flying Stars, the ones you are born under and those stars that change annually.

Chapter Five

Flying Stars

One of the systems used within Feng Shui is called Flying Stars. I've mentioned them a few times. This chapter will explain what they are and how they are applied. They are a great tool to help my clients, and I use them alongside other Feng Shui techniques to bring abundance into their lives.

You may notice some repetition in this chapter. The stars are the same whether you are born under them or whether they are the annual Flying Stars. However, the way they impact us is different, and the way we use them is not the same. So that you can understand them better, I have used repetition to help you get acquainted with the terms (there is also information I have shared in other chapters) to enable you to check the details to understand them properly.

Flying Stars influence our lives on two levels. We are each born under a Flying Star, and, every year, each star falls into a different area of our homes and offices.

There are nine Flying Stars in total. They are:

White Water Star 1
Black Earth Star 2
Jade Wood Star 3
Green Wood Star 4
Yellow Earth Star 5
White Metal Star 6
Red Earth Star 7
White Earth Star 8
Purple Fire Star 9

As you can see from this list, each Flying Star is also associated with an element. There are four earth stars, two wood stars, one of each metal, water, and fire star. These elements can help to activate the area they fall into in any given year. However, you will only want to activate them if they've fallen into a favourable area.

As you will remember, the areas of our homes and offices each have an element. Those elements are shown in the information accompanying the descriptions of the nine areas on the Lo Shu Grid in Chapter Two. These elements are critical to being able to activate the areas you most associate with abundance. Each also has a supporting element and elements that will clash with the element associated with that area.

For example, the West of our house is metal. If you want to activate or support it, use earthy tones, but don't use wood furniture or decorations because that will affect the flow.

The centre is earth, so I always recommend keeping it neutral, quiet, and uncluttered.

Below I have listed the elements for each of the areas of our homes and the supporting and clashing elements.

South-East	South	South-West
4	9	2
Element: Wood	Element: Fire	Element: Earth
Supporting Element: Water	Supporting Element: Wood	Supporting Element: Fire
Clashing Element: Metal	Clashing Element: Water	Clashing Element: Wood
East	Centre	West
3	5	7
Element: Wood	Element: Earth	Element: Metal
Supporting Element: Water	Keep Quiet	Supporting Element: Earth
Clashing Element: Metal	Clashing Element: Wood	Clashing Element: Fire
North-East	North	North-West
8	1	6
Element: Earth	Element: Water	Element: Metal
Supporting Element: Fire	Supporting Element: Metal	Supporting Element: Earth
Clashing Element: Wood	Clashing Element: Earth	Clashing Element: Fire

The Flying Stars also represent different aspects of our lives.

White Water Star 1 – Career and New Beginnings
Black Earth Star 2 – Relationships
Jade Wood Star 3 – Romance and Ancestry
Green Wood Star 4 – Good Fortune
Yellow Earth Star 5 – Well-being
White Metal Star 6 – Helpful People
Red Earth Star 7 – Creativity and Children
White Earth Star 8 – Wealth and Knowledge
Purple Fire Star 9 – Fame and Illumination

Before we get to the annual Flying Stars, let's talk about the Flying Stars we are born under.

Flying Stars – Birth

The only way to know which star you fall under is to have a session with someone like me who can map your year, month, day, and time of birth.

However, here's what you need to know if you are **born** under these stars:

1. White Water Star 1

This star is a water element and happily represents opportunities, success, and recognition in your career. Good news! If you were born under this star, it's considered auspicious, and you can influence it to be even more favourable. What do I mean by that? If you use it properly, career growth, promotions, and overall success at work could be yours. Sound good?

That's great, but I guess you want to know how. Harnessing the auspicious energy is relatively straightforward. First, you need to know where the 1 Star is in the Lo Shu Grid. If you look at the Lo Shu Grid for 2024 (you can find all of the grids at the back of this book), you will see that the 1 Star is in the East. Because Star 1 is a water element, you can activate its energy by placing moving water in the East.

I have often used fish tanks or some other sort of water feature for clients born under Star 1. If the East falls outside your home, you can have a pond or even a small fountain. But don't use solar power because this represents the fire element, which should not be used with water. Metal is an excellent way of increasing the energy of water because, as I've mentioned before, metal is a supporting element for water.

If you were born under a White Star 1, your best years are likely to occur when your 1 Star interacts with or falls in the areas 1, 6, 8, or 4 on the Lo Shu Grid. Check out the yearly charts at the back of the book to find out when your Star 1 falls into one of these areas. In 2025 it will fall into the South-East.

2. Black Earth Star 2

Star 2 is an earth element. If you don't handle this star properly, it can mean challenges in your life and sometimes even misfortune. When this star appears in an area of your home or office, it can negatively influence various parts of your life, including health, relationships, and wealth.

Wherever this appears, you need to drain the area. To do this, you must place many metal objects in the space. Keep this area clean and decluttered. Make sure it stays quiet and calm in whatever part of your house/office it appears in any given year.

In 2024 Star 2 falls into the South-East, so this is the area to focus on keeping clean, uncluttered, and quiet. In 2025 it will move to the centre of your home or office. This is the area where, in general, I encourage people to focus on keeping decluttered and quiet.

3. Jade Wood Star 3

If you were born under the Jade Star 3, then good news—this star brings good fortune, prosperity, and abundance. It's all about growth, success, and opportunities in a range of areas in your life, including wealth, career, and personal endeavours.

Wherever the star appears in your home or office in any given area, it is considered highly favourable. It can really contribute to bringing you positive outcomes and achievements. Happy days!

Star 3 element is wood, and the supporting element is water, so you can apply both to increase the energy and benefit of this star. Water features and plants will help you get the best out of this area, and you can also use the colour blue.

In the Flying Stars grid for 2024 you will see in the East, which is Jade Wood Star 3, that the Flying Star for that year is 1 White Water Star. This is auspicious as it is all about opportunities: 'when one door shuts another one opens'. In 2025, the 9 Purple Star Flying Star enters and this one is all about Fame and Illumination.

4. Green Wood Star 4

Being born with Star 4 generally means you will have an auspicious life as it is definitely a positive star. Its element is wood, and it's associated with growth, creativity, and academic pursuits. You have been born with vitality, expansion, and abundance. That sounds pretty good, right?

When Star 4 is in an area of your home or office, it brings favourable energy to support your educational pursuits, artistic endeavours, and personal development. You need moving water to activate this energy to make the most of it. Inside that means water features and fish tanks. If it falls outside your home, you can use ponds or fountains. Do not use solar-powered water features in this area.

The best years to use are those when Star 4 falls into areas 4, 3, 8, or 1. In 2024 Star 4 will be in the North-West, and in 2025, it will fall into the West.

5. Yellow Earth Star 5

If you're born under Star 5, life will be a roller coaster. You are in for a very interesting ride. What do I mean by that? Sometimes this star can be inauspicious, but when things are good, they are very good. However, you might not want to get out of bed when they're not great.

It can be a challenging star, for sure. It's associated with disruptions, obstacles, and potential setbacks. But the upside is that it will make you much stronger, particularly in your dealings with people.

There are remedies you can use in your home or office, but for you personally, I recommend wearing greys, whites, and reds as a form of protection. It can also help to have regular clearing and massages to move any stagnant Chi or energy, which will disperse the negativity.

In 2024 Star 5 will fall into the West, and in 2025, it will be in the North-East. Just keep these areas quiet.

6. White Metal Star 6

You are blessed with good fortune if you are born under this star. You have an increased ability to be successful in your life. It can give you favourable energy, not only in your career advancement and financial success, but also in your overall well-being. It can bring recognition and wealth as well.

If you're looking for professional success, leadership roles, and financial stability, then you need to align your home or office yearly using the different energies for that year.

In 2024 Star 6 is in the North-East, and in 2025 it will move to the South. You can activate these areas with music, fire, and the colour red.

7. Red Earth Star 7

This is a very interesting star to be born under. It's not the most auspicious star, but you can counterbalance its effect. It can be associated with conflicts, theft, and betrayal. As such, it can be known as the Robbery or Violent Star.

When Star 7 is present in your life or falls into a part of your house or office, it can bring challenging energy that can manifest as arguments, legal issues, or a loss of wealth.

The upside is that those born under this star can be party animals. They love to have fun and are very popular with their friends and family. People can't help falling in love with them.

Use fiery bright reds, oranges, and yellows in this area to support the earth element.

In 2024 this challenging star will be in the South, and in the following year, 2025, it will be in the North.

8. White Earth Star 8

This is a very fortunate star and auspicious. Number 8 is associated with wealth, prosperity, and good luck. It's about abundance with financial and business success, and can positively impact your life.

In Chinese culture, the number 8 is pronounced similarly to the word for 'wealth' and 'prosperity' in various Chinese dialects, which indicates that it's a strong number in China.

Star 8 is earth energy, stable and balanced energy. The supporting element is fire, so use bright reds, oranges, and yellows here. The downside to Star 8 is that you may put on weight more quickly.

In 2024 you will find this auspicious star in the North, and in 2025, it will shift to the South-West. You can activate this area with water.

9. Purple Fire Star 9

This is one magical star to be born under. You can manifest anything you want. You do need to remember, though, that manifesting is only part of the formula for success; you must also take action.

Star 9 is associated with future prosperity, expansion, and overall good fortune. It is the fire element and is often referred to as the Multiplying or Magnifying Star—you can see how that would be a good thing!

When Star 9 falls into an area of your home or office, it brings favourable energy to attract wealth accumulation, success, and overall abundance. We could all use a bit more of that!

I generally put my manifestation boards together using Flying Stars each year, and I have a section on how to make one of these boards in my chapter on Mindset and Manifestation.

Ensure you activate this star wherever it falls in your home or office every year. In 2024 it will be in the South-West, and in 2025, it will move to the East. You can activate with fire in 2024 and water in 2025.

Flying Stars – Annual

As well as our year of birth, Flying Stars also impact our lives in the **area** they appear in any given year. They reside there throughout the entire year. There are other stars which change monthly, daily, and hourly. Still, we will concentrate on the annual changes, as they are the most significant. Again, there is some repetition in some of the details from the stars you are born under, but they affect your life differently.

This may seem complicated at the moment, but once you get the hang of it, you will be able to Feng Shui your house or office yearly, and keep the energies flowing and up to date.

Let me show you what I mean by Flying Stars in the Lo Shu Grid. Every year, starting in the Chinese New Year, the nine stars fall into different grid areas, affecting those areas of our homes and offices.

Below is the Lo Shu Grid for 2024.

2024

South East	South	South West
4 2	9 7	2 9
East 3 1	**Health** 5 3	**West** 7 5
North East 8 6	North 1 8	North West 6 4

You will see that the areas of your home remain the same (they are represented by the larger numbers and stay the same every year). The second, smaller numbers are the Flying Stars for 2024 and will only remain in these positions for the Year of the Wood Dragon from February 10, 2024, ending on January 29, 2025, when the Wood Snake will come into play.

What do these stars mean for the areas they fall into each year?

1. White Water Star 1
When this star is in an auspicious or favourable area of your home or office, and it is activated, you can expect great things to happen in your career—growth, promotions, and success. Star 1

is also all about new beginnings, so you can be sure that if one door closes, another will open.

The best years to use Star 1 are when it appears in a box whose areas contain 1, 4, 6, or 8. Avoid activating this star when it's in box 5. When that happens, keep this area quiet, calm, and uncluttered.

How can you activate this star when it's in an auspicious area? Colours work, so use blues, greys, white and black. Symbolism or pictures of water can really help. But choose paintings of tranquil waters, not storms, unless you want some upheaval in this area of your life.

Water features work well to activate the energy of this star. Fish tanks and indoor water features are great. If this area falls outside, you can go all out and have ponds or water fountains to get the energy flowing. One warning, do not use solar power to light or power these water features because that will work against what you're trying to achieve.

2. Black Earth Star 2

This star is all about relationships and wealth. It can be an inauspicious star, which means if it's not managed properly, it can cause some stagnation and negative energy in whatever area of your house it's in. That's particularly relevant if it's in a box whose areas contain 2, 5, 3, or 7. If not handled properly, it can go as far as causing misfortune.

But if it's linked to 4, 6, 8, or 9 in the grid's boxes for the year, you can activate it to bring yourself good fortune. When you do this helpful people can appear in your life.

How can you activate this star? The best colours for this area are bright reds, oranges, and yellows. Whatever you put into this area as decoration, use groups of two—two red candles, two yellow cushions, or two orange flowers.

This area is about relationships, so the symbolism revolves around couples looking loved up and happy. Don't put up paintings of three people or a single person. The focus needs to be on two happy people together.

3. Jade Wood Star 3

This is an auspicious star. But if used wrongly, it can be inauspicious, so read this advice carefully. It's a star relating to good fortune, prosperity, and abundance. Activated properly, you can attract growth and opportunities to your wealth, career, and personal endeavours.

Activate this area when the star appears in the boxes for the year showing 1, 3, 4, 6, 8, and 9. Do NOT activate it when it's in a box with 2, 5, or 7.

As it's important to get this one right, here is my advice about activating it. Use blue, brown, and green in this space. Water features are amazing in this area when this star appears in the box with 1, 3, 4, and 9, so feel free to use fish tanks and indoor water features here in those years.

Decorate the area with pictures of your family, ancestors, and trees.

4. Green Wood Star 4

This a very auspicious star to activate in its usual space in the South-East of your home. When the star appears in a box with 1, 4, 6, 8, or 9, you can activate it and get the energy flowing, bringing you wealth, good fortune, fame, helpful people, and career change. If you are self-employed, then you can expect substantial positive changes. The best years to use these stars are those when it lands in a box with 1, 4, 6, 8, and 9. These are the best times to activate it. But keep the area calm when the 4 Star winds up in areas 2, 5, and 7.

Star 4 is all about growth, creativity, and academic pursuits, and these areas can provide abundance in many forms. If this star appears in an area of your home or office, it can bring very favourable energy to your educational, artistic, and personal development ambitions.

How should you activate it? Use moving water—inside means water features and fish tanks; outside, you can go for broke and put in ponds and fabulous water fountains. Don't use solar power; it will obstruct the energy you're trying to activate. Using colours blue, green and teal on wooden lamps and soft furnishings such as curtains and cushions will enhance this area. Symbolically, as this is a wood area, pictures of trees, bamboo, horseshoes, and elephants with their truck upwards facing the door would work well here.

5. Yellow Earth Star 5

This is one of the most inauspicious stars. I recommend that my clients refrain from activating the energy in whatever area this appears in any given year, or they will attract disruptions, struggles, obstacles, and potential setbacks. You may also struggle to communicate with people because they won't understand where you are coming from.

If you choose to activate this area or do this by accident, then 'Life Is a Rollercoaster' will be your year's anthem. The good news is there is a way to avoid activating it—do NOT drill or renovate this area of your house or office. This is especially true if this star appears with another 5 in the same box, which will be the centre of your home or business. Put down the tools!

The element in this area is earth. Don't add anything. Keep it quiet and tranquil for an easier life. Placing metal in this area will help to drain the negative energies of the yellow star.

6. White Metal Star 6

This is one of my favourite stars. It's all about bringing helpful people into your life. It's a powerful area. When the annual Flying Stars 1, 4, 6, 8, or 9 are in the same box as the White Metal

Star you can expect career changes, promotions, good fortune, and massive support from friends, family, and even the odd stranger. It can even influence wealth and fame.

But do not activate the area when it falls into the same box as 2, 3, 5, or 7. This will attract robberies, sicknesses, anxiety, and legal problems.

The element for this star is metal which means you can use earth to support the area. Consider putting in some plants with rounded edges. The symbolism for this area is helping people, so put pictures of people you'd like to help you, whether they are friends, family, colleagues, or acquaintances. Anyone you think could help you with your career or even make you famous.

The best colours are whites, purples, pinks, and greys. Concentrate on putting pictures in this area of people that inspire you. It also is a great area for travel pictures and spiritual influences.

Suppose it's professional success you're looking for through leadership roles or financial stability. In that case, you must align your home and office annually using the changing Flying Star energies.

7. Red Earth Star 7

It is only wise to activate this naughty star if it has auspicious stars to outweigh the negativity. This star is all about creativity and fun, but only activate it when it shares a Lo Shu box with Annual Flying Stars 1, 4, 6, 8, or 9. In these years, it will bring you new beginnings, good fortune, helpful people, wealth, fame, and the icing on the cake, inner peace.

But suppose you try to activate it when it shares a box with 2, 3, 5, or 7. In that case, you can expect illness, legal problems, anxiety, and robberies.

The element is earth for this star, which is supported by fire, so use bright fiery colours like reds, oranges, and yellows to support your growth. Avoid wood, or you could find yourself with too many decisions and risking making the wrong one.

8. White Earth Star 8

This amazing star brings with it the chance of wealth, prosperity, and great luck. This is an area I often activate for my clients within their homes and offices.

If Star 8 falls into a Lo Shu box with 1, 3, 4, 6, 8, or 9, then I would activate it by placing water in that area of your home. I do not mean a cup of water but large quantities like an aquarium. But do not activate it when it shares a box with 2, 5, or 7, or you will attract calamity, illness, or robberies.

The element for this area is earth. Earth is supported by fire, so use bright reds, oranges, and yellows in this area. The symbolism is wealth, so put luxury furnishings into this area and aim to create a feeling of abundance. Avoid wood and metal in this area as much as possible.

9. Purple Fire Star 9

This is a very auspicious star and will bring success and overall abundance into your life.

You should activate it when it appears with a 1, 3, 4, 6, 8, or 9. This will attract promotions, great entrepreneurial success, good fortune, romance, wealth, helpful people, fame, good relationships, and even the chance to get your family together.

Always avoid activating the Purple Fire Star if it sits with a 2, 5, or 7 star, or calamity will find its way to you. It can mean you get stabbed in the back by a friend or colleague (not physically, unless you have extraordinary friends), and robberies.

The element is fire, so avoid water or, as you can imagine, your dreams will fizzle out. Use reds, golds, purples, and oranges in this space. Symbolism in this area involves paintings of famous people or images that remind you of spirituality or inner peace.

If you want to know what the Flying Stars are from 2025 onwards, check out the Lo Shu Grids and the cheat sheet I've prepared for you at the back of this book. Now you will learn how to interpret the grid and which areas to activate, and what spaces to keep calm and quiet and how.

There are many helpful tools that can help you activate energy in your chosen areas, and I will tell you about some of them in Chapter Six.

Chapter Six

Useful Feng Shui Tools

Now that you know about the Bagua Map, Lo Shu Grid, and the Flying Stars, I want to share some of the key tools you might need to activate more positive energy in your house, office, or garden.

Decluttering

As you will notice as you read this book, decluttering is a big deal in Feng Shui. If you want energy or Chi to flow through your house freely, then obstacles and mess will not help. It's like putting physical barriers between you and your goal.

There is no end of decluttering tips on the Internet if you search, but I wanted to share with you the ones that have brought about the best results for my clients when working on their homes and offices, and for me in mine.

It's just about working out what you need and what you have. The difference between the two is what shouldn't be there.

I used to buy haphazardly and whatever made me happy on the day I was shopping. Now I'm a declutter freak. I always think twice before I buy something. Do I need it? Why do I need it? Or will it just make me feel good in the brief moment I buy it? These days I will even leave a shop to think about an item, and if I still think I need it, I will go back and buy it.

The old me would literally have to come home with as many shopping bags as I could carry, but not anymore!

Simple Decluttering Ideas

So many of us have moved in with someone and found that we have two of so many items. Nobody needs two sets of glasses, cutlery, or crockery. Just have a frank discussion and choose those that suit you both best. You can argue if you must, but then use the ten-minute rule—you must make up after ten minutes.

Ultimately, decluttering is about organising. We all do it. We use something, scissors, for example, but don't put them back where they belong afterwards. Whenever you go from one room to another, keep an eye out for items in the wrong place and put them back in the right place as you move around the house. You will then get in the habit of not leaving items around. That's the plan, anyway.

Bathrooms with multiple shampoos, soaps, conditioners, and toothpaste—I know, you get the picture—use one at a time. Once it's finished, then replace it. Deals like buy one, get one free are only bargains if we use them, and they don't just become clutter. I had one client who had ten boxes of tea in case she had guests.

Washing has to be done and kept in one area, whether you have a big or small family or home. Spreading it around and cluttering the rest of your house won't help anyone, and will affect the areas of your life where the clutter is. Get everyone to put their washing in whatever area you choose. When it's washed and ironed, put it away immediately, don't just leave it lying around. It's clutter, whether it's clean or dirty. Your family might get better at it if they know that their income, success, career, or school marks depend on it. They might be up for trying harder.

The same goes for the dishes. Everyone leaves them in the sink at some point. Wash them up and put them away immediately. The upside is that you won't have to clean two-day-old dishes or put your hands into dirty dishwater, which is gross. Do it every day.

Wardrobes

I can tell you this is a big one, and I'm not immune to a messy wardrobe. I promise never to let it get messy again every time

I tidy it, but however hard I try, three months later, it's a mess. But I practise what I preach and clear it out again. A little bit like *Groundhog Day*, but I'm motivated by knowing what amazing changes it makes for my life and the lives of my clients.

A lot of my clients find decluttering their wardrobes challenging, so while it isn't strictly Feng Shui, there are certainly some methods out there on how to declutter your clothes I wanted to share with you. This is the process that I use.

I take all the clothes out and divide them into categories—tops, jumpers, dresses, trousers, and coats. I consider each item individually and decide whether I will wear it next week. It goes back into the cleared-out wardrobe if it's a clear yes. If it's a definite no, it's off to the charity shop. If I'm unsure, I pop it into a bag, put it away for six months, and then revisit it.

This doesn't take as long as it sounds because it never builds up much over three months. It's so satisfying to have a clear wardrobe, and it keeps the positive energy flowing in that part of my house.

There are so many upsides to this. When I first started practising Feng Shui, I realised I had clothes I loved that I'd forgotten. On the flip side, I also cringed at some impulse buys and happily sent them to the charity shop to become someone else's 'treasure'.

One great tip is to turn all your hangers the wrong way around. As you wear them, turn the hanger the right way around. If you haven't turned the hanger the right way around after six months, then off to the charity shop it goes.

I also use the Three-Box Method to declutter every room in my house. I have three boxes (or bags) labelled donate, sell, or rubbish.

Desk

I have a drawer in my desk where I chuck everything—pens, elastic bands, loyalty cards, print cartridges, diaries, coins, sunglasses, just about anything that doesn't belong elsewhere if I'm honest.

Now and then, that drawer gets too full and annoys me so much that I decide to declutter it, just like the wardrobe. However, I'm much harder on the drawer. Anything I don't use ends up at a charity shop or thrown out. There's a good chance that if those things don't have a place, you don't need them.

Kitchen Cupboard

You've heard about some of the areas I'm rubbish at, but my kitchen is my strong point. My partner will tell you that I hate out-of-date food. If you look in my cupboards, the chances are you won't find anything that is even a single day out-of-date.

But like everyone, I like to declutter my cupboards sometimes to know what I have been buying at markets or on days out. I start by removing everything from the cupboard and then clean it out.

I check the expiration date of all the food items. If I find something that is in date, but I'm not going to use it, then I give it away.

My cupboards are organised into canned items, oils, snacks, and sauces. My partner likes to organise everything alphabetically, so cayenne is always in front of the chilli. I use clear plastic containers to keep cereals, flour, and rice with clear labels. Like so many people, I put heavy items on the bottom shelves of my cupboards. I put my new items behind the older ones to reduce the chance of waste when I'm unpacking the shopping.

One of my cupboards is filled with items I use all the time. That makes accessing what I need quick and easy, especially when I'm in a hurry. I can throw together a healthy meal in 25 minutes. I like to have a seasonal shelf in this cupboard. I don't drink hot chocolate in summer, so it's replaced by things I will need.

Doors

Front doors are the mouth of our houses, so they should always be kept clean and freshly painted. This will ensure that the Feng Shui of your home or office is balanced and harmonious, allowing the positive Chi to flow through your home.

The magic comes when you choose an auspicious or favourable colour for your door. Here are my recommendations for great colours to use depending on what direction they face.

North

If your front door faces North, choose beautiful blues and bold blacks; this will positively impact your career and work opportunities.

North-East

This is the door of wealth and knowledge. You have a few colours to choose from — try burgundy, reds, crimsons, or earthy colours.

East

East is the door of romance and family. So, if you want abundance in love for you and your people, enhance the Chi with green or blue. Any shade of green is perfect here, so you can choose whatever you want, from subtle sage to fabulous forest green.

South-East

This is the door of good fortune. Here a wooden door would attract more positive Chi than a plastic one. I would paint this door in your favourite shade of blue. While painting it, think about what good fortune means to you.

South

South-facing doors are all about fame, so hit it with rich red or classy crimson to attract those opportunities through your front door. A south-facing door can't be a wallflower red; it must be 'in your face' red.

South-West

These doors are about relationships, and to match the variety of relationships you can have, the colours that work here are also diverse. You can choose a tasty terracotta, an awesome orange, brilliant yellow or even pretty pink.

West

If your door faces West, it's all about creativity. To get your creative juices flowing, enhance the great Chi by choosing winter white, elegant grey or passionate purple. This door can also be about children, so if you want to engage in that sort of creation, use one of these colours to bring abundant energy through your door.

North-West

If your door faces North-West, it's all about bringing Helpful People into your life, and we all need a few of those! To enhance the positive chi entering the house choose a fresh white as this is associated with new beginnings, or a sophisticated grey for pure elegance.

Mirrors

Placing your mirrors is seriously important in your home and office. They move positive energy around the house to make sure that there are no stagnant energy areas, so they must be put in the best possible places. They are like windows. When they're placed correctly, they can lighten up your life in your home.

The key point regarding mirrors is that they reflect whatever comes into your life. So, using mirrors to reflect outside your home is like bringing positive energy in from the outside.

As you come through your front door, it's always astute to have one on the sidewall as you open the door. Fresh air hits the mirror and sends powerful energy around the house.

One easy strategy is to place mirrors opposite windows wherever possible. This allows you to reflect the positive energy outside.

There are different materials for mirror frames and other shapes you can use. Here are some tips for which mirror shapes to place in various areas of your house and what they will bring to the eight life areas. We want to keep the centre quiet and calm, so I haven't mentioned it here.

- Round mirrors in the South-East and North-East bring Prosperity and Abundance.
- Square mirrors in the West and North-West will attract Creativity and Helpful People.
- Triangular or pointing mirrors in the East and the South-East bring Romance and Good Fortune.
- Unusual or quirky mirrors in the South bring in Fame and Illumination.
- Curvy Mirrors in the North will allow your life to flow positively.
- I don't like mirrors that are in three parts. You will only be able to see part of yourself in each of these sections. This depicts change, but not in a positive way. You must see yourself clearly in any mirror, whatever shape you choose.

Don't put mirrors on show in the bedroom because your soul needs to sleep. They are very active furniture to have in your home, and your bedroom needs to be calm and bring harmony to help with relaxing and a good night's sleep. For that same reason, don't have a TV.

If you need a mirror in your bedroom, consider putting one on the inside door of the wardrobe, which means you can close it away. This is what I do in my house.

A tip when you hang mirrors is to ensure you can always see your entire head and shoulders. If you don't do this, you could have multiple headaches.

TV & Music Systems

Televisions and music systems are very active furniture to have in your home, and your bedroom needs to be calm. So don't have them in there.

Place them in rooms in the West, North-West or North. You can place them in the South, but you will be too engrossed in Netflix to go to bed. Never put them in the South-West as that is the relationship area, and that area must be all about the two of you with no outside influences.

Water Features

We've talked about Feng Shui meaning wind and water. Using water to activate an area of your home or office is potent if you've cleaned and decluttered first.

How Much Water Do You Need?

I'm often asked that. A cup? No, it's not enough. A pitcher of water? Still not enough. But a fish tank is enough. It doesn't have to have fish, but the water must have a pump and be moving. I have a fish tank in my house with no fish, and it looks really pretty.

A swimming pool is excellent, but you only need it for a year, so consider a temporary, above-ground one. Keep it clean—not for Feng Shui reasons—stagnant pool water is unlikely to activate anything other than nasty bugs and viruses.

A pond is also more than enough, but will you put one in for a year? If you have a missing space, for example, in the South-East, which is good fortune, then a pond for life is positive.

Water features inside like fish tanks don't have to be expensive. I've even used a large, tall bucket, put a fish tank pump with an aerator in the water, and placed it in the area I want to activate. I've also used a bucket with a fish tank pump and aerator stone.

Your objective is a large amount of moving water; and a quick tip: if your dog uses it to drink, make sure you keep topping it up.

I often get asked whether you can put more than one water feature in your home or office. Yes, I usually choose a few to activate those auspicious areas in any given part of my home or my clients' homes.

Command Positions

Command positions refer to the best place to put essential furniture in your home or office to get the best results.

Cooker or Oven

Your cooker or oven represents the element of fire, known as the heart of the family. The best place for this in your home is in the South of your kitchen. The second-best place is the South-West of your kitchen.

Try not to put your kitchen sink within two feet of your cooker because everything fizzles when fire and water meet. That will affect the life area where the oven is situated. You don't want to lose all your money.

Avoid placing your cooker in the North or North-West of your kitchen. You don't want to stop helpful people from coming into your life or new opportunities from turning up.

Bed

The commanding position for your bed is diagonally from the door. You need to be able to see the door from your sleeping position, but you don't want your feet facing it. They call this the coffin sleep.

If you have insomnia, try to place your bed so that the top of your head faces North. They call this 'the sleep of the dead', and it will stop nightmares. I often use this when a child has trouble sleeping.

If you're in a relationship, have the top of your head facing East for more romance.

If creativity is important to you, have the top of your head facing West.

Avoid South; only a few people can sleep with their heads facing this way; too much fire will keep you awake. But if it's passion you're looking for, then you can spend a few nights with the top of your head facing South.

Desk

There are two options when it comes to the placement of your desk. The best place is in the North-West with your back to the wall and facing at an angle to the window, if you have a window. This isn't always possible as you may have a bedroom or living room in this part of your home. So, my second suggestion is to have your desk facing a window and bring in fresh air.

Desk Set-up Using Feng Shui

- Think of your desk as a mini Bagua Map with the nine life areas. Place your phone to the right of you in easy reach.
- Place your computer/laptop in the centre of your desk with your keyboard in front of it.
- Place your credit card machines to the left of you and keep them there when you are working on finances or with chequebooks.
- Pictures of your true love (no children, family, or dogs) should be placed at the top right corner.

- Any light or lamp should be on the top right. Make sure it's a bright light. You don't want anything dull in that space.
- Put your files and books away at the end of every day.
- The rest of your desk should be kept uncluttered—get rid of your empty coffee cups, half-eaten sandwiches, perfume, lipstick, and anything else that doesn't need to be there.

Space Clearing

Space clearing has a significant role in Feng Shui. It can be used to create, harmonise, and balance your environment.

We've all walked into a room where the energy just feels wrong. We might feel uncomfortable but not know why. The chances are that you're picking up on negative energy. But where does that negative energy come from?

There are so many reasons for a room to feel like this. It could be from people arguing there, someone who might have passed away, or the energy might have become stagnant because no one spends time there.

You can use space clearing to eliminate negative and stagnant energy, and to restore positive, flowing energy back into the room. Space clearing can enhance positive energy by creating a more vibrant and uplifting atmosphere.

That's great, but how do you actually do it?

You'll need some sage. I've found American sage the best, but others are on the market. You'll also need a bell, matches, and a plate.

First, move around your house in a clockwise direction ringing the bell. Make sure you open cupboards and ring your bell in and behind doors. Don't miss any small areas when you're doing this. That will ensure there is no negative or stagnant energy left behind.

Next, you need to light your sage and carry a plate underneath it—it won't improve the experience if you burn holes in your carpet or leave marks on your floorboards.

Wave your sage throughout your whole house, walking clockwise around it. At this point, it's vital to clarify your intention while doing this.

What Do I Mean by Clarifying Your Intention?

We use our intention to manifest change and to put positive energy into our home or office. Think about what you want your future to look and feel like. What changes do you want to see in your life? This is the time to set your goals for the future and dream big.

Finish off the space clearing by waving the sage over yourself from top to bottom, covering yourself in positive energy.

Once you've done this, your home will be revitalised, and you'll be ready to enjoy all the positive energy you've created.

Candles

Candles are super aligned to Feng Shui and, unsurprisingly, represent the element of fire. You'll remember we've talked about the five elements in Feng Shui—Fire, Earth, Metal, Water and Wood.

Fire represents illumination and transformation. When you use candles in the right area, they can create harmony and vibrant energy. They are used during meditation; setting your intentions; goal setting; or when performing Feng Shui rituals or activating an area of your home or office.

Red candles symbolise passion and recognition. Place them in the South to enhance your fame and reputation.

Pink or White candles are all about love, purity, and harmony. Put them in the South-West, which is your relationship area.

Green candles represent growth and abundance. They attract prosperity when you use them in the East and South-East of your property, which is Good Fortune.

Purple candles symbolise spirituality, wisdom, and introspection. The North-East of your home/office is about wealth, but it's also all about knowledge and wisdom. If you are studying or want to meditate, this is the best area to place them.

White candles symbolise purity and clarity, and enhance psychic abilities. Place them in the West and North-West, especially if you are trying to solve problems.

Blue candles placed in the North symbolise communication and have healing energies. Suppose you have something to say but need help communicating it. Sit quietly in the North and think of the person. Picture the ideal conversation in your mind. When the opportunity arises, the discussion will flow more positively.

Candles are only a small activation, unlike large amounts of water. Still, they can bring subtle and beneficial changes to your life, and, as you can see from above, they also have a symbolic purpose.

Crystals

I don't use crystals in Feng Shui to activate areas of our homes or offices, but they have their place. They are used to enhance the flow of positive energy.

Different crystals have different vibrations that can influence the energy in the room. While this is not an area I often use in my work as a Feng Shui Consultant, they are fascinating and can enhance positive energy. And I'm all about creating more positive energy.

Crystals for wealth and abundance are citrine or pyrite, and should be placed in the North-East of your home or office.

The South-East and East is the area for love and relationships, so use rose quartz or amethyst. They are said to promote love, harmony, and romance.

The South is for clarity and focus. Clear quartz crystals in your home or office help you focus and concentrate.

Placing black tourmaline or hematite crystals in the North of your house, near windows or doors, will absorb negative energy and provide protection.

Place amethyst in the West and North-West of your home to enhance your intuition and create a calming energy. This crystal also resonates with metal; as the West and North-West are the metal elements, it will reinforce these areas.

In the South-West of your home, the relationship area, place rose quartz. It is the crystal of love, compassion, and harmony in relationships.

Little crystal cluster trees are available, and they radiate positive energy. Place these crystals in bathrooms and toilets.

Crystal mobiles and wind chimes can be placed outside or near windows and doorways to disperse positive energy around the house.

Although this is not strictly Feng Shui, many people choose to carry crystals with them, not only because they are beautiful but because of the energy they promote.

It is important to cleanse and recharge your crystals to remove any negative energy they have absorbed. Do this by placing them outside on a full moon and a new moon.

Crystals in Feng Shui are about symbolism, personal belief, and intention; they aren't used to activate any of the nine areas of the Lo Shu; however, they have their place.

Yin and Yang

Another integral part of Feng Shui is Yin and Yang. Using these energies in your home can bring amazing results. The concept of Yin and Yang has been around for centuries. It is referred to in many different ways, but ultimately, Yin and Yang are about duality, balance, and interconnectedness. They refer to different energies that are inseparable.

Yin

Yin represents feminine energy. It is associated with stillness, softness, gentleness, calmness, and darkness. In Feng Shui, we use this energy for relaxation and introspection. The South-West (Relationships) and North-East (Wealth/Knowledge) are excellent areas to use Yin symbolism.

Yin symbolism is all about subdued lighting, soft textures, and luxurious colours like deep burgundy reds and golds. Symbolic shapes to use in these areas are circles and cylinders. The seasons related to Yin are winter and spring. Yin is elementally cold.

Yang

Yang represents male energy. It is associated with activity, assertiveness, speed, movement, strength, and dynamic energy. The areas to activate for Yang energy are the South which brings fame and illumination, and the North-West, which brings in the male energy; this space in our home is where the father's energy lives. The North-West, when activated, also brings helpful people into your life.

Elementally, Yang is hot. The symbolic shapes to use are triangles, squares, and rectangles. Squares and rectangles are also used with the Earth element.

What is valuable to remember is that balance is important and that specific areas of the house relate to Yin or Yang energy. To get the most out of them, use symbolic colours and shapes to enhance their impact.

These tools help you activate the energy in your home. In the next chapter, I will share with you some common mistakes people make.

Chapter Seven

Common Mistakes

Let's talk about common mistakes people make that affect the positive energy in their homes and offices.

Before we go into each of the areas, there is one rule that covers everywhere, and that is decluttering. We want the energy in our bodies to flow freely, and we want the same for our homes and offices. Anything that causes an obstacle or blocks the flow of positive Chi will slow things down and even cause stagnation. Whatever abundance means to you—you don't want it stagnating or slowing down to a crawl. Not clearing clutter is, far and away, the most common mistake people make in their homes and offices.

North

As you know, the North of our homes and offices are about our career and success. The North is the water element and is particularly important as it's the only water element area. Avoid the fire element because it opposes the North. We all know what happens when we combine water and fire—it all ends up in a fizzle. I'm guessing if someone asked you about your career, you wouldn't want to have to describe it as having fizzled out!

You need to avoid bright colours in the North such as red, orange, and yellow as these fire-like colours ideally give all bright colours a miss in this area. If you want to put up artwork, go for water-themed images and colours like seascapes, boats, and lakes.

Don't put heavy furniture in this area because it will slow your career energy down. You don't want to let anything stand in the way of getting the job you want. Avoid big plants or wooden furniture for the same reason. The North of your home is the only water element in your whole house, and the flow of energy starts from here, so you really don't want anything to slow it down.

If your granny gave you her Victorian mahogany dining table, don't keep it there, or you'll be waiting years for the promotion you've been angling for. Just shift it to the East. Your granny will be more than happy with that.

North-East

The North-East is about wealth and knowledge, and its element is Earth. The most important thing to know here is that you must avoid excessive metal, or it will weaken your finances, and nobody wants that unless you've won the lottery recently. Avoid sharp objects because they represent the wood element, and having them here will affect your capacity to take knowledge in.

Unless you're a supermodel, you might want to avoid having heavy furniture in this area because it might mean you gain weight. Don't put your fridge in that area—as the old saying goes, 'fridge pickers wear big knickers'. It doesn't have to be a fridge, but I'd definitely leave heavy furniture out of the North-East.

It's super important not to have obstructions in this area. Don't use water here. Adding water to an earth element means everything gets soggy, sludgy and murky. It will make your money and wealth area stale, and, much worse than that, it can mean that someone might steal your money.

East

The East is about romance and ancestry, and the element is wood. Don't use fire here because it will suppress the energy. It will render the wood energy ineffective. Using a lot of metal here can mean you have difficult decisions and could go down the wrong road. This area is all about growth and expansion, so you need to add water to it to help nourish it.

Lighting a fire is the biggest mistake you could make in this area. That will cause arguments in your extended family. It may sound basic but don't put pictures of people you don't like in this area. If you must put up a picture of your Grandpa Walter, don't put it here unless you want his influence in that part of your home.

If there is a fireplace in the area, don't light it. Don't keep metal in the East—if you have your ironing board in there, move it to the West, North-West or North.

South-East

We've talked about good fortune, which means different things to everyone. Whatever it means to you, follow similar rules to the East because the South-East is also a wood element sector. So, don't use fireplaces or fire in this area. Fire and wood are not a great mix. Unsurprisingly, fire drains the wood energy.

Avoid excess metal, as this will impact your decision-making about good fortune. This area also affects legal matters, so don't keep your bills in that part of your house or office, or you'll end up paying your bills forever. If you put fire colours in there, you can expect legal problems. If you're buying a house and everything is going well, lighting up the fire or putting a fire-related image in that area will cause the sales chain to fall apart.

Nobody can have too much good fortune, so use water to support that area. Use a water feature with a large amount of water or a fish tank. I recommend two goldfish for energy and luck, and one black fish for protection. Fish will activate the positive Chi of that area but don't use a fish tank in your bedroom or the South of your home.

South

The South is all about fame and illumination. The element in this sector of the house is fire. It's no surprise that you shouldn't use water in this area. If you do, then if you asked me, 'When will I be famous?' I can tell you that the answer is never. Avoid water in this area, or you can forget ever finding yourself on the red carpet.

You can use wood to add to the positive Chi in the South. Put up pictures of famous people in this area. As I mentioned earlier, I have a picture of *Fight Club*, not only of Brad Pitt, but signed by him, up on my wall.

Avoid pictures of shipwrecks. This can have the effect of you finding yourself alone or on your own amongst people that aren't like you. You could be the only 'plain digestive' in a box of 'chocolate hobnobs'. People can find themselves very lonely. Pictures of famous people or films are always a good choice here, but make sure they reflect positive Chi. *Jaws* would be a no-no.

South-West

The South-West of our homes is all about our relationships; the element is Earth. Avoid wood, as it can cause arguments. Don't use items with threes in them or three of a particular object unless you want a third party in your relationship. Any pictures must only be of the two of you. Don't put up photos in this area with anyone else in them—not even your kids or pets. If you put up pictures for decoration, make them of a happy couple on a beach or walking through Paris together. Have two of everything you use in that part of your home—two swans, vases, or red candles. If you have a table in that part of the house, make sure it's a table for two so you reinforce the energy of your relationship. If you're lonely, don't put up images of people alone, even if they look happy and like they're having fun.

Avoid water and metal in this area, or you might meet someone who isn't what they say they are. Don't use black here; stick with reds, oranges, and yellows. Don't use heavy furniture; you want to keep the energy light and breezy. I don't recommend having a TV in this area, or your partner's attention won't be on you. But you can have gentle music playing here.

Unless you want a third person interfering in your relationship, don't have a picture of your mother-in-law in that part of the house, or she might move in with you.

West

The West of our homes is all about creativity and children; the element is Metal. Avoid wood, or you won't want to pick up your paintbrush or pen. You'll find your ideas and inspiration drain away. Although it's a metal area, don't use too much of it because it can affect your ability to have children. Avoid anything that reminds you of people or times that weren't happy.

Put up things you love that will motivate you. I love clocks so I have them in the West of my home. All of my furry family pet pictures are on the walls. Elephants are good luck, but don't put a wooden one in this area; glass and metal are okay. Avoid wooden frames for pictures. Metal frames are better. Avoid sloths, though, because they do not represent motivation or creativity. Avoid harsh lighting in this area, or it could stifle your creativity.

North-West

The North-West has Metal as its element and is all about helpful people and travel. Avoid fire in this area because it will affect your positive Chi. Using fire means that you will attract the wrong people into your life. The chances are they will be dominant and take you in a direction you won't want to go in. If you use wood here, you could find yourself the piggy in the middle of a power battle. Water in this space can also mean you will come across as totally self-interested and egotistical to other people. Don't use bright colours here.

Use glass and more tranquil colours, or you may become someone you wouldn't want to spend time with or be with people who aren't right for you.

Centre

The centre of our house is about well-being. For many of us, the centre is where our stairs are, unless you live in a flat or a bungalow. There can be a few problems with that. Where we need free-flowing energy, we can tend to use the space underneath as a space to store odds and ends, anything that doesn't have another place to go. I was forever leaving stuff at the bottom of mine to take with me when I went upstairs, although I do that less now. This can result in the centre of our homes being constantly cluttered, and let's be serious—it's not great for our well-being if we're tripping over things at the bottom of the steps.

Don't just drop things in the centre of your home or leave them there. I tend to clean room by room and collect items I need to take back upstairs or downstairs, so the bottom of my steps becomes a pile of stuff. Keep it clear and put things where they belong.

As we know, the centre of our homes is an earth element, so don't put any metal or wood objects in this space. They will clash with the Earth; keep it tranquil and quiet. Don't play music or have radios or televisions in this space. What we need for well-being is peace and quiet. You can't heal yourself by activating this space, but you can certainly keep it calm.

In the days when everyone had landline telephones, this was often the place they used to keep them. Many of us only have mobiles, but if you still have a landline, there are better places for it. Think about it—if you're on the phone with your partner and they annoy the hell out of you, the energy of that conflict will stay in this space. It will mess with your peaceful energy.

In the next chapter, I'm going to talk about Chinese Astrology and Feng Shui.

Chapter Eight

Chinese Astrology and Feng Shui

Chinese Astrology and Feng Shui are rooted in Chinese culture and share many common elements. Using them together they will complement each other, giving a feeling of well-being and creating harmony in different areas of your life.

Both take a holistic approach, considering the interconnectedness between individuals and their homes or offices. Chinese Astrology examines a person's own energy from their date of birth. Feng Shui focuses on the relationship between the energy of spaces where the occupants live and work.

The Yin and Yang elements of Fire, Earth, Metal, Wood, and Water are represented in different areas of the nine sectors of the house.

North – Water
North-East – Earth
East – Wood
South-East – Wood
South – Fire
South-West – Earth
West – Metal
North-West – Metal
Centre – Earth

There are 12 Chinese animals, and each animal also has an element.

Rat – Water
Ox – Earth

Tiger – Wood

Rabbit – Wood

Dragon – Earth

Snake – Fire

Horse – Fire

Goat – Earth

Monkey – Metal

Rooster – Metal

Dog – Earth

Pig – Water

Each year the positive energy in our lives changes. That's why my clients have personal readings for the coming Chinese year. We are born under a Flying Star, and our home has Flying Stars, and as we go into each year, we can prepare ourselves to optimise the positive energies for the year. Using the information from our Chinese Astrology chart for the year alongside Feng Shui and the annual Flying Stars, we can maximise the potential of the auspicious and favourable parts of our life and home.

So, let's join the dots. Each Chinese animal has a place in their home or office where they feel comfortable, and so do their friends.

Chinese animal	Area of home/office	Element	Friends
Rat	North	Water	Ox, Dragon, Monkey
Ox	North-East	Earth	Rat, Snake, Rooster
Tiger	North-East	Wood	Rabbit, Horse, Pig
Rabbit	East	Wood	Goat, Dog, Pig
Dragon	South-East	Earth	Rat, Monkey, Snake
Snake	South-East	Fire	Ox, Monkey, Rooster
Horse	South	Fire	Tiger, Goat, Dog
Goat	South-West	Earth	Horse, Rabbit, Pig
Monkey	South-West	Metal	Rat, Dragon, Snake
Rooster	West	Metal	Ox, Snake, Dragon
Dog	North-West	Earth	Tiger, Horse, Rabbit
Pig	North-West	Water	Tiger, Goat, Rabbit

It's not unusual for people to buy a home built in one of the years that is auspicious for them. For example, Rooster buys a house built in 1929, the year of the Snake.

Can You Use Your Chinese Animal to Activate Energy?

No, you can't use your Chinese animal to help activate areas of your home. You can certainly use water features and decluttering, as discussed in other parts of this book. However, remember to check the location of the most auspicious areas for the year, and the annual Flying Stars residing there at that time.

Each Chinese animal has a friend (see the chart above), and if you spend time in the areas they are linked to, you will get the feel-good factor.

Secret Friends

Every animal also has a secret friend which connects to a different area, as you can see in the list above. A secret friend can come in all forms, mentors, friends, family, or a stranger who comes into your life briefly. It's always worth asking people their year of birth so you get a heads up whether they are likely to be friends or someone you're likely to clash with.

Let me explain the difference between a friend and a secret friend. A friend is someone we want in our life and enjoy their company. A secret friend might come into your life to teach you a lesson. They might be a boss you don't like, but you become better at your job under their guidance. They are not someone you would want to spend your free time with, but they play a valuable role in teaching you something important.

Rat = North
Ox = North-East
Tiger = North-East
Rabbit = East
Dragon = South-East

Ox = North-East
Rat = North
Pig = North-West
Dog = North-West
Rooster = West

Snake = South-East   Monkey = South-West
Horse = South   Goat = South-West
Goat = South-West   Horse = South
Monkey = South-West Snake = South-East
Rooster = West   Dragon = South-East
Dog = North-West   Rabbit = East
Pig = North-West   Tiger = North-East

When I refer to clashes in Chinese Astrology and Feng Shui, I'm referring to some areas in your house that you might feel less comfortable in. They're not negative spaces, but they aren't where you feel most comfortable in your home. This has more to do with the energy or Chi we have as human beings born under specific signs—some we will simply gel with more than others.

I have also listed your clashes. Does that mean they are foes rather than friends? No, it doesn't, but you can be sure they will stretch your patience and teach you lessons about yourself.

Rat = North   Horse = South
Ox = North-East   Goat = South-West
Tiger = North-East   Monkey = South-West
Rabbit = East   Rooster = West
Dragon = South-East   Dog = North-West
Snake = South-East   Pig = North-East

According to your Chinese animal, these are the auspicious hours when you will be at your best for anything you want to achieve:

Rat   07.00–09.00 & 15.00–17.00
Ox   09.00–11.00 & 17.00–19.00
Tiger   11.00–15.00 & 19.00–23.00
Rabbit 05.00–07.00 & 19.00–23.00

Dragon	07.00–09.00 & 15.00–19.00
Snake	09.00–11.00 & 15.00–19.00
Horse	11.00–15.00 & 19.00–21.00
Goat	11.00–15.00 & 21.00–23.00
Monkey	07.00–11.00 & 15.00–17.00
Dog	11.00–15.00 & 19.00–23.00
Pig	13.00–15.00 & 19.00–23.00

2024 Year of the Dragon – Activating Abundance

2024 is the Year of the Dragon. You can use the Flying Stars chart to see where the most auspicious areas will be throughout the year. You need to do this every year to see which are the most favourable areas.

In 2024, the most auspicious areas are the following:

North, where the Rat is positioned, which will hold the wealth star.

South-West, where the Monkey is situated in the relationship area, has a manifesting star. This will help you manifest the partner you want, but you will need to take action to help it along.

East is where the Rabbit is positioned and has both the career and new beginnings star and the manifest star, which you can activate with water.

However, you will need to avoid the West where the Rooster sits, as it has the Yellow Earth 5 Star. Although the Rooster is the Dragon's secret friend, you must keep this area quiet and calm, or you will have a roller coaster of a year.

Which Chinese Astrology Animal Are You?

You can determine which Chinese animal you are born under using your year of birth. There's one caveat to that. The Chinese year starts later than our Western calendar year. So, if you were born in 1969, you would usually be a Rooster, but if you were born before Monday, 17th February 1969, you would actually be a Monkey. A simple online search can tell you on which day the Chinese New Year started in the year you were born.

For each of the Chinese animals listed below please refer to the dates when the Chinese New Year fell in any particular year. If you were born very close to the date of the Chinese New Year you are likely to exhibit traits of both the outgoing, and incoming, animal of the year.

Rat – the Action Animal
Rats were born in the years 1900, 1912, 1924, 1936, 1948, 1960, 1972, 1984, 1996, 2008, or 2020.

Let me tell you a bit more about Rats. You are lucky in love, and happily, you're blessed with great looks. You are very sociable and love a party, but an introvert is also hidden in there. Everyone needs a little time by themselves, after all. That said, you won't like not being around people for extended periods. Being alone for long will make you feel very low and can lead to depression.

You are mega opinionated and outspoken, especially when it comes to something you feel strongly about; politics, cruelty, and injustice, to name just a few. These issues will also bring out your sensitive side. You are highly intuitive and often sense things before they happen.

Ox – the Trustworthy Animal
If you were born after the Chinese New Year in 1901, 1913, 1925, 1937, 1949, 1961, 1973, 1985, 1997, 2009, or 2021.

There's lots to love about an Ox. You're a hard worker, thoughtful, and laid-back. People trust you because you are kind and can be trusted. For this reason, you are also a great leader, as you're good at making decisions.

You're not easily stressed. You take everything in your stride. But that's where the decision-making comes in—you won't commit until you've thought everything through.

You can be introverted and don't fancy being the centre of attention, but you're not a wallflower. You prefer a relaxed night out at a pub in your jeans to a fancy party.

Tiger – the Hunter

People born after the Chinese New Year in 1902, 1914, 1926, 1938, 1950, 1962, 1974, 1986, 1998, 2010, or 2022.

Tigers! You're confident, direct, and outspoken, and you probably wouldn't be surprised if people thought you were full of yourself. However, under all of that is a gentle soul.

You're passionate and driven, and will be good at whatever you choose to put your effort into. You'll be irritated by anyone not pulling their weight, and can feel a bit down if you don't get your way. That said, you will always listen and take on other people's opinions, regroup and bounce back.

Freedom of choice is important to you, and you're well-known for being a risk-taker. Tigers don't tend to take much downtime. They are always looking for the next opportunity. Having said that, you do know how to relax. A good book will help, but there's every chance you'll choose a self-help book to enable you to go out and get what you want.

Rabbit – the Kind Animal

You would be a Rabbit if you were born in 1903, 1915, 1927, 1939, 1951, 1963, 1975, 1987, 1999, 2011, or 2023.

Rabbits have kind, generous and forgiving natures and will do anything for anyone. Unfortunately, the downside is that you are a sensitive soul who can take things to heart.

You are a great friend, and for Rabbits, family is everything. You will invest a huge amount of your time in your relationships, and when people do not reciprocate, you feel abandoned. You are a party animal and can keep going until the early morning hours, but you must balance that with time by yourself and rest.

Dragon – the Oracle

Dragons were or will be born after the Chinese New Year in 1904, 1916, 1928, 1940, 1952, 1964, 1976, 1988, 2000, 2012, or 2024.

People want to be around Dragons all of the time. You can hold an entire room's attention. You will mesmerise the people in it when you talk about something you're passionate about.

Your life will be full. You're driven and ambitious and will put in the work to achieve your goals. That, and your enthusiasm, will get you exactly where you want to be and put money in your pocket along the way. You're an action-taker and achiever with confidence and charm mixed in. I don't need to tell you that you're an extrovert with a strong sense of justice, which can make you oversensitive.

Snake – the Intuitive Animal

Snakes were or will be born in 1905, 1917, 1929, 1941, 1953, 1965, 1977, 1989, 2001, 2013, or 2025.

You might be the most sensitive of all the Chinese animal signs. You're also intelligent, intuitive, and a stickler for being on time. You would never have found yourself in detention at school.

You are a deep thinker, patient, and plan everything. Added to that, you are super intuitive. You spend a lot of your time silent, patiently waiting and observing. Risk-taking is not in your DNA.

You may be a bit shy and introverted, even though you may come across as an extrovert to others.

Horse – the Leader

You would be a Horse if you were born in 1906, 1918, 1930, 1942, 1954, 1966, 1978, 1990, 2002, 2014, and 2026.

Wow, you're lucky—good-looking, lucky in love, sociable, and super charismatic. You have the gift of the gab, and everyone wants to chat with you. That might have something to do with how charming you are.

You're determined, unphased by anything but can be stubborn. Sometimes you need to take other people's advice, but that won't come easily and can trip you up.

You have a way of attracting the right people into your life, and people can't help falling in love with you. Lucky for them, you are a passionate lover. Horses are sensitive and not selfish. You do like being around other people but really need some time alone in case you burn out.

Goat – the Peace-making Animal

You would be a Goat if you were born in 1907, 1919, 1931, 1943, 1955, 1967, 1979, 1991, 2003, 2015, and 2027.

You are the negotiator of the Chinese animals because you are patient and trustworthy. You always see two sides to each story. People need to beware that if they take your kindness for granted, they may well regret it. You love being around people and are great company, but you'd choose smaller groups over a big party.

You like being liked and can be a bit insecure if you feel ignored or criticised, but don't we all? You can also be introverted, and because you are so sensitive, you may choose to spend more time on your own.

You like to go with the flow, and you're a veritable intuitive peacemaker who can be a great listener if you put your mind to it.

Monkey – the Sensitive Animal

If you're born in 1908, 1920, 1932, 1944, 1956, 1968, 1980, 1992, 2004, 2016, and 2028.

You're talented, creative, and quick-witted. You also can be cunning and devious. You are fun to be around but can be pushy and opinionated. Like Dragons, fairness and justice are critically important, and you will fight hard for the underdog every time because of your sensitive soul.

You can give great advice, step up, and be there for those you love in troubled times. Adventure, curiosity, and imagination are all a big part of your life and will inspire you in whatever path you choose. Beware that you don't spend too much time in the real world, though.

Rooster – the Rule-breaker

If you were or will be born in 1909, 1921, 1933, 1945, 1957, 1969, 1981, 1993, 2005, 2017, or 2029, you're a Rooster, but only if you were born after the Chinese New Year.

Roosters are reliable, trustworthy, and direct. You work hard, and you'll meet your deadlines because you're super conscientious and methodical. You're often better working for yourself, but if you decide to take a high-level position in a company, you'll be great at it.

You're super stylish, and people can't help falling in love with you. You're extroverted and opinionated when needed, and you've likely been a bit of a rule-breaker in your time. You love a party and being sociable but are good at getting the balance with time at home as well.

You shine on social occasions, and people cannot help themselves by being impressed by you.

Dog – the Trustworthy Animal

Dogs were born, or will be born, after the Chinese New Year in 1910, 1922, 1934, 1946, 1958, 1970, 1982, 1994, 2006, 2018, and 2030.

It's probably no surprise that Dogs are faithful, loyal, and protective. You can be cautious, particularly when you're making decisions. You are strong-willed and stubborn, and definitely no fan of change. You might be introverted, but in your quiet way, you are very opinionated.

You're not particularly sensitive but can be emotional. Of all Chinese animals, you are the one people can most rely on and trust, and you enjoy serving and helping others. If you're given a task, you will not only make it happen, but you'll enjoy doing it.

You can be good at studying and hit dizzying heights in your chosen field.

Pig – the Wise Animal

Pigs were born, or will be born, after the Chinese New Year in 1911, 1923, 1935, 1947, 1959, 1971, 1983, 1995, 2007, 2019, or 2031.

You're logical, honest, and good-natured, and you love having fun. On the flip side, you take your obligations very seriously, in your personal life and at work, and you have a lot of empathy. You're unlikely to be surprised that you have a touch of OCD and need everything in its place.

You are completely honest, but you're not one for arguing if you can avoid it. In fact, you might be the peacemaker in a group or the one who calms troubled waters. You like a bit of indulgence, but you make sure those you care about don't go without. People will fall in love with your mind and heart.

Following on from this chapter on Chinese Astrology, I'm going to share with you the elements we are influenced by depending on the year we were born in.

Chapter Nine

Your Birth Element and How to Use It

The year you are born has an element attached to it. Check out the chart at the end of this chapter, which will tell you which you were born under. This element relates to your personality. Using this element in your charts and the elements in your home or office helps bring the two together. Here are some ideas on how to do this.

If you live with other people, I recommend focusing on your element as you are the person using Feng Shui to enhance the positive energy in your home. If there is a room that only one person uses, then you can use their element in that room.

Fire Element

There are two types of fire elements—Yang and Yin. Yang is more outgoing, and Yin is a gentler energy. There are some common traits between them, such as being passionate, with loads of energy, and you can find it hard to chill out. You have both vibrant and dynamic energy, which you can use to get what you want.

Fire people like being surrounded by family, friends, and colleagues, although you like your chill-out time. If you are at a party, look for the person that is the centre of attention. They're bound to be a fire person. Fire element people are charismatic and are like magnets, and you will draw people to you.

You are best suited to sales and marketing. However, you can become actors/actresses, DJs, or any role in the public eye or on stage. You can take on leadership roles, and those working with you will be inspired by your work ethic and ability to share your knowledge and support people around you.

You are optimistic, although you can be a bit sensitive, even if that's not obvious to you. You're passionate about love and life. You guard your freedom. Tying a fire person down can be hard, so marriage isn't always on the cards. Alternatively, you may find yourself with more than one marriage under your belt.

Using Your Fire Element in Your Home

The shapes to use are triangles which are associated with the element of fire with their upward-pointing shapes. Angular shapes like diamonds or pyramids work as well.

If you are placing plants in this area, make sure they have petal leaves that come to a point like the Mother Tongue plant.

Crystals in the form of pyramids are excellent. Rubies, orange calcite, and other vibrant options bring motivation when they're placed in the South of your home or office. The best colours to use are greens, reds, browns, and bright oranges.

Pictures should be of sunsets, sunflowers, and vibrant abstract pictures. Remember that the Horse in Chinese Astrology sits in the South. Using images to symbolise horses is perfect here. The best crystal for this area is fire agate which is associated with transformation, motivation, and courage. You can use wood and fire in the South to enhance positive energy.

Careers that work for you are sales and marketing, the entertainment industry, and event management as you bring your passion for fun to life. You can hold leadership and management positions as you have a way with people.

Earth Element

People born with the Yang earth element are grounded and stable. You can sometimes feel a bit stuck. You're super compatible with a Yang fire element person who can help you become unstuck. Yang earth people are reliable, patient, and trustworthy. You will never let anyone down intentionally. You have a practical outlook on life and provide stability in life's storms.

Earth people love their food and can be known to overeat. I recommend that earth people ensure the North-East of your home is not over cluttered, or that can result in you putting on weight. The good news is that if you keep this area neat and tidy and use manifestation and action, you can find your missing waistline.

You love romance and a steady relationship and want to avoid conflict at home and work. If there is too much conflict, you will retire into your shell and become silent and withdrawn. If you feel a little low, wear red and sit next to an open fire until you are ready to face the world again. Using fire in the North-East and South-West can help activate positive energy.

Using Your Earth Element in Your Home

The symbolic shapes for this area are squares, cubes, and rectangles. These shapes symbolise stability and give a strong foundation to your life. The supporting element of earth is fire, so use colours like red, orange, yellow, and earthy colours.

The best pictures would be symbols of abundance, harvest, landscapes, mountains, and anything else resembling strength and stability.

The best crystal for this area is moss agate, which represents energy and growth, and promotes ground and stability to the earth.

Earth people make amazing landscape architects, gardeners, environmental conservationists, and teachers to name just a few.

Metal Element

If you're born in the year of Yang or Yin metal you are ambitious, strong-willed, and determined, and can be a bit OCD when it comes to your home and work. You are competitive and like to win. You're super self-reliant, and you genuinely don't think you need support from anyone. Finding yourself an earth person who can support you when you go into creative overload is hugely beneficial. They will be the type to bring you a hot drink and sandwich when you desperately need it.

You are searching for success and will give yourself almighty goals and move any obstacles in your way. You can bounce back after setbacks because you don't believe anyone who tells you something can't be done. That will be like a red rag to a bull, and you'll put 110% effort into proving them wrong.

You can be a bit self-obsessed, but you won't realise it until someone you love points it out gently. You love to laugh and have fun, but you're generally in bed before the clock strikes midnight. You will excel in the legal profession or anything creative.

Using Your Metal Element in Your Home

Metal should be used in the West and North-West of your home. The best shapes to use are round and circular. Round mirrors are a great example. Spherical shapes represent unity and balance. You could use six balls in the North-West to bring helpful people into your life.

You can use metal statues of elephants with their trunks facing outwards. This is believed to be lucky. Six coins tied together with a red ribbon placed at 330 degrees is auspicious for wealth in this area.

The support element for metal is earth. So, plants in terracotta pots with round leaves work well. The picture symbolism could be a Monkey or Rooster as their Chinese element is metal. Pictures of musical instruments or landscapes are great here to represent metal and earth.

The best crystal for this area is clear quartz. It amplifies your energy, brings clarity to your life, and helps you focus.

Law, legal work, engineering, technology, architecture, Feng Shui, project management and research are all great for metal element people. Metal people like precision so finance and auditing are also great careers for them.

Water Element

You are the most sensitive of the five elements and can be a bit unpredictable. Your emotions tend to flow like water. The upside is that you are adaptable and flexible.

People born under the water element are the best to contact if you have a problem because they are intuitive and understand other people's emotions, much like an empath. You are particularly empathetic to other people's needs.

You are full of the wisdom of someone who has lived 1000 lives. You're happy to share your knowledge with anyone, even if they don't want to listen.

You love to travel because being in the same place doesn't work for you. Your moods can change on a whim, and people may find it hard to keep up. If you are looking for a relationship, slow down long enough to work out what you really want out of life and then go for it. With your positive intentions, anything is possible. Careers working with people, travel, IT, and anything musical will work for you.

Use a water feature in the North to enhance positive energy.

Using Your Water Element in Your Home

The shapes that work best for this element are flowing, like waves. You can use spherical shapes which represent the flow of water. Think of gentle zigzags or twists and bends in a flowing river.

I recommend Yin and Yang signs as it shows perpetual motion. Water landscape and pictures of goldfish (eight gold and one black) work well. You may have seen these in Chinese restaurants and takeaways. Pictures of waterfalls and gentle rivers flowing enhance the water element.

Dolphins or sea turtles symbolise the water element and promote harmony. The supporting element is metal for water, so use metal objects and water features.

The best colours to use are grey, white, blue, and purple. The most favourable crystal is aquamarine which gives off calming and relaxing energy, and will help you with clarity for any decisions you need to make. Aquamarine is also used for emotional healing.

Writing and journalism are great jobs because those born under the water element are amazing storytellers. Research and analysis, environmental science, especially jobs with anything to do with oceans or bodies of water, are great. You will also do well in arts and music.

Wood Element

You love to talk if you are Yang wood. If you're Yin wood, you represent growth and expansion. I call you innovators as you have hugely creative minds and come up with new ideas.

You inspire others at work. Whether you are in a job, self-employed, or employed, you can get other people motivated. It's your superpower.

There's no reason for you not to be in a relationship if you want one. You are a great networker. People find you interesting and sometimes unusual. In a relationship, you tend to take the lead as you like to organise trips and parties. You like any gathering, whether it's work or play. You do need to listen more, though! If you do, you will make excellent counsellors and rise to giddy heights, thanks to your excellent networking skills.

You will need to drink a lot of water or spend time near water, or you will feel drained, and no amount of sleep will compensate for the loss of energy.

Using Your Wood Element in Your Home

The best shapes for the wood element are rectangular, vertical, and upward, like a tree. They are shapes of growth and structure. If these shapes are made of wood, that will bring even more vitality and growth into your life.

The element that supports wood is water. You can use tall vases with water and flowers, preferably blue, for example, Bluebells or Forget-me-nots. The colours for this area are blues, browns, and aqua greens.

The best crystal for this element is jade which is associated with wisdom and harmony. You can use a water feature in the East and South-East to help activate this element.

Teaching, education, counselling, social work, psychology, and management positions where you are able to support others are great for you because wood people help others grow.

In the next chapter, we will talk about the importance of using mindset and manifestation alongside Feng Shui to attract abundance into your life.

Year	Element
January 30, 1930 - February 16, 1931	Metal, yang
February 17, 1931 - February 5, 1932	Metal, yin
February 6, 1932 - January 25, 1933	Water, yang
January 26, 1933 - February 13, 1934	Water, yin
February 14, 1934 - February 3, 1935	Wood, yang
February 4, 1935 - January 23, 1936	Wood, yin
January 24, 1936 - February 10, 1937	Fire, yang
February 11, 1937 - January 30, 1938	Fire, yin
January 31, 1938 - February 18, 1939	Earth, yang
February 19, 1939 - February 7, 1940	Earth, yin
February 8, 1940 - January 26, 1941	Metal, yang
January 27, 1941 - February 14, 1942	Metal, yin
February 15, 1942 - February 4, 1943	Water, yang
February 5, 1943 - January 24, 1944	Water, yin
January 25, 1944 - February 12, 1945	Wood, yang
February 13, 1945 - February 1, 1946	Wood, yin
February 2, 1946 - January 21, 1947	Fire, yang
January 22, 1947 - February 9, 1948	Fire, yin
February 10, 1948 - January 28, 1949	Earth, yang
January 29, 1949 - February 16, 1950	Earth, yin
February 17, 1950 - February 5, 1951	Metal, yang
February 6, 1951 - January 26, 1952	Metal, yin
January 27, 1952 - February 13, 1953	Water, yang
February 14, 1953 - February 2, 1954	Water, yin
February 3, 1954 - January 23, 1955	Wood, yang
January 24, 1955 - February 11, 1956	Wood, yin
February 12, 1956 - January 30, 1957	Fire, yang
January 31, 1957 - February 17, 1958	Fire, yin
February 18, 1958 - February 7, 1959	Earth, yang
February 8, 1959 - January 27, 1960	Earth, yin
January 28, 1960 - February 14, 1961	Metal, yang
February 15, 1961 - February 4, 1962	Metal, yin
February 5, 1962 - January 24, 1963	Water, yang
January 25, 1963 - February 12, 1964	Water, yin
February 13, 1964 - February 1, 1965	Wood, yang
February 2, 1965 - February 20, 1966	Wood, yin
February 21, 1966 - February 8, 1967	Fire, yang
February 9, 1967 - January 29, 1968	Fire, yin
January 30, 1968 - February 16, 1969	Earth, yang
February 17, 1969 - February 5, 1970	Earth, yin
February 6, 1970 - January 26, 1971	Metal, yang
January 27, 1971 - February 14, 1972	Metal, yin
February 15, 1972 - February 2, 1973	Water, yang
February 3, 1973 - January 22, 1974	Water, yin
January 23, 1974 - February 10, 1975	Wood, yang
February 11, 1975 - January 30, 1976	Wood, yin
January 31, 1976 - February 17, 1977	Fire, yang
February 18, 1977 - February 6, 1978	Fire, yin

February 7, 1978 - January 27, 1979		Earth, yang
January 28, 1979 - February 15, 1980		Earth, yin
February 16, 1980 - February 4, 1981		Metal, yang
February 5, 1981 - January 24, 1982		Metal, yin
January 25, 1982 - February 12, 1983		Water, yang
February 13, 1983 - February 27, 1984		Water, yin
February 28, 1984 - February 19, 1985		Wood, yang
February 20, 1985 - February 8, 1986		Wood, yin
February 9, 1986 - January 28, 1987		Fire, yang
January 29, 1987 - February 16, 1988		Fire, yin
February 17, 1988 - February 5, 1989		Earth, yang
February 6, 1989 - January 26, 1990		Earth, yin
January 27, 1990 - February 14, 1991		Metal, yang
February 15, 1991 - February 3, 1992		Metal, yin
February 4, 1992 - January 22, 1993		Water, yang
January 23, 1993 - February 9, 1994		Water, yin
February 10, 1994 - January 30, 1995		Wood, yang
January 31, 1995 - February 18, 1996		Wood, yin
February 19, 1996 - February 6, 1997		Fire, yang
February 7, 1997 - January 27, 1998		Fire, yin
January 28, 1998 - February 15, 1999		Earth, yang
February 16, 1999 - February 4, 2000		Earth, yin
February 5, 2000 - January 23, 2001		Metal, yang
January 24, 2001 - February 11, 2002		Metal, yin
February 12, 2002 - January 31, 2003		Water, yang
February 1, 2003 - January 21, 2004		Water, yin
January 22, 2004 - February 8, 2005		Wood, yang
February 9, 2005 - January 28, 2006		Wood, yin
January 29, 2006 - February 17, 2007		Fire, yang
February 18, 2007 - February 6, 2008		Fire, yin
February 7, 2008 - January 25, 2009		Earth, yang
January 26, 2009 - February 13, 2010		Earth, yin
February 14, 2010 - February 2, 2011		Metal, yang
February 3, 2011 - January 22, 2012		Metal, yin
January 23, 2012 - February 9, 2013		Water, yang
February 10, 2013 - January 30, 2014		Water, yin
January 31, 2014 - February 18, 2015		Wood, yang
February 19, 2015 - February 7, 2016		Wood, yin
February 8, 2016 - January 27, 2017		Fire, yang
January 28, 2017 - February 15, 2018		Fire, yin
February 16, 2018 - February 4, 2019		Earth, yang
February 5, 2019 - January 24, 2020		Earth, yin
January 25, 2020 - February 11, 2021		Metal, yang
February 12, 2021 - January 31, 2022		Metal, yin
February 1, 2022 - January 21, 2023		Water, yang
January 22, 2023 - February 9, 2024		Water, yin
February 10, 2024 - January 28, 2025		Wood, yang
January 29, 2025 - February 16, 2026		Wood, yin
February 17, 2026 - February 6, 2027		Fire, yang

February 7, 2027	-	January 25, 2028	Fire, yin
January 26, 2028	-	February 12, 2029	Earth, yang
February 13, 2029	-	February 1, 2030	Earth, yin
February 2, 2030	-	February 22, 2031	Metal, yang
February 23, 2031	-	February 10, 2032	Metal, yin
February 11, 2032	-	January 30, 2033	Water, yang
January 31, 2033	-	February 18, 2034	Water, yin

Chapter Ten

Mindset and Manifestation

Mindset and Manifestation

I can give you all the advice you need to activate the areas of your home and office, but its success will be limited if you have the wrong mindset and don't use manifestation. I teach both to my one-to-one and group clients to maximise their results. This makes an enormous difference.

Getting rid of obstacles, decluttering, and activating the areas of your house will go a long way to achieving your goals, but true and sustainable abundance comes to those who optimise their results with mindset and manifestation.

Here I explain the principles of what I do with my clients. You may already be familiar with the concepts. They're not new, but they are powerful.

Mindset

What do I mean when I talk about mindset? Your mind can influence how you see things or perceive the challenges in your life. A positive mindset refers to approaching goals or hurdles optimistically. It's not always easy but seeing obstacles as learning experiences is an example of a positive mindset. It doesn't mean we don't feel grumpy, down, or even afraid sometimes, but we get back up and move forward anyway. This type of mindset can be critical to us when using Feng Shui to attract positive energy and manifest change in our lives.

If you want to manifest change, then the answer is to align your mind and thinking to your dreams, with no doubt about what you want to happen. Let me give you an example: you want to buy a new white car. You haven't noticed white cars, and you wonder who else drives one. You start to think about this, focus on it, and boom, your mind delivers; suddenly, you see white cars and their owners everywhere.

I've seen this happen with people who want something really badly. Take prospective authors. If they are stuck in a negative mindset, they will think everyone is writing books and no one ever gets publishing deals. Suppose they face the challenge of getting published with a positive mindset. In that case, they will suddenly see authors getting agents and publishing deals. They will feel as if opportunities surround them.

Why Is Mindset So Important?

You can follow this book and attract positive energy into your home or office, but if you are operating from a negative mindset, you yourself will bring negative energy into your space. You can see how that would be crazy. You'd be working against your own ends.

Having a positive mindset allows you to ensure your dreams come true. Living with a negative mindset can make you unhappy, whereas a positive mindset attracts more positive energy. You know that positive energy will attract abundance into your life, so why not reinforce Feng Shui with your positivity?

When you feel as if everything in your life is going wrong, the energy you put out is, 'What will be next? My life is so bad.' That is what the universe hears, and then you will attract more of the same. As you start to use gratitude and see the good things in your life, that is when you will begin to attract what you want, and the magic happens.

What Sort of Mindset Do You Need?

You need to be aware of what is going on around you. You need to be clear about what you want from your life and what abundance means to you.

Once you've decided what abundance means to you, start thinking about how you can physically achieve it and then take action towards it. This is the formula for an abundant life.

Dream + Feng Shui + Mindset + Manifestation + Action = Abundance

How Does Mindset Work alongside Feng Shui?

If the formula for an abundant life is Dream + Feng Shui + Mindset + Manifestation + Action = Abundance, imagine what happens when you add positive energy through Feng Shui and a positive attitude. You can move faster towards your goals and achieve so much more when you add positive energy into the mix and remove obstacles and negative or stagnant energy.

When you use Feng Shui and a positive mindset with the tools I've given you in this book relating to the nine sections of your home, you will achieve abundance, whatever that looks like to you.

Let me give you an example. Suppose you wanted to change your career, which is in the life area in the North of your home. In that case, you need to work on using the tools I've given you in this book, such as decluttering, colours, and elements, to attract positive energy. For the best results, and why would you want anything else, you must have a positive mindset and manifest the life you want.

Get your mind to do the work, it is one of the most underestimated parts of our body, yet it holds the key to our dreams and ambitions.

Manifestation

This brings us to manifestation. What do I mean by manifestation? It refers to creating or attracting your goals and dreams by using intention. You need to believe that your thoughts, beliefs, and energy influence the world around you and that you can shape your experience.

Our goals will happen when we align our thoughts, emotions, and actions. I want to reiterate and emphasise action because nothing you want will happen without taking action.

You can create a manifestation board with your dream house, a cheque for £1 million, a loving partner, or beautiful children, but nothing will happen without you taking action. To win the lottery, you must buy a ticket, right? If you want to meet someone wonderful, you have to put yourself out there to meet someone; they're unlikely to walk into your home. If you want to have children—well, you get the picture. The point is that action is a compulsory part of the process.

You need to set your intention for your dream house, and then go and find it. The universe will have heard you when you said you wanted it, and it will steer you in the right direction, but it can't pick you up and put you directly in front of it.

Setting your intention, manifesting that goal or dream, and then taking action will help you attain your goal.

How Does Manifestation Work with Feng Shui?

It works in exactly the same way as it does with a positive mindset. You need to use manifestation—you can use manifestation boards, journals, meditation, or visualisation alongside the Feng Shui tools in the nine life areas of your home to attract abundance into your life.

How Do I Help My Clients to Manifest Abundance?

I am asked this a lot. When we have our consultation, we run through exactly what they want in their lives. I then identify the areas in their homes and offices that are best to activate physically to achieve that. While working in this area, I ask them to visualise or imagine exactly what they want.

If they're working in the good fortune area, in the South-East, I will get them to declutter and clean first, and whilst they are doing that, I ask them to think about exactly what they want in a positive way. I help them identify colours and other tools as well as using symbolism for this area, while taking its supporting elements into account. I identify the Flying Star they are born under and the annual Flying Stars to ensure we take full advantage of the positive stars and neutralise any negative ones. If there are auspicious stars in the South-East that year, I would ask them to place a water feature in that area. Inside I would recommend a water feature like a fish tank. If it falls outside, it could be a pond or water fountain. But it must not be solar powered because it must run constantly. However, a critical factor in attracting the most positive energy for the life they want comes from manifesting and keeping a positive mindset.

One of the most powerful tools is a manifestation board. Here's how you can create one.

Creating a Manifestation Board
Every year, around the Chinese New Year I make a manifestation board using the Feng Shui Lo Shu Grid.

Why Do I Recommend Manifestation Boards?
Manifestation boards are a great tool to help provide clarity in terms of your goals, desires, and intentions for the year ahead.

We have talked about the tools of visualisation, manifesting, and intention, and how powerful they are. Creating this board and placing it in an auspicious area each year brings positive energy into our lives.

The Feng Shui Manifestation Board is a visual reminder every day to keep you aligned with your personal intention, and as I always say, you need to take action in line with your goals for the year.

Creating our boards aligns with the principles of the Law of Attraction. The Law of Attraction states that positive thoughts and attention can attract positive experiences and outcomes.

How Do You Make a Manifestation Board?

There are different ways of making a manifestation board. Some of the clients I work with prefer their manifestation boards in a digital form so they can look at it on their screen savers on their phone or computer.

Others prefer a hard copy, but they also have different style preferences. Some prefer to use words only, and others like pictures. It is important that you use what works for you. You're the one who needs to want to look at it and focus on your goals for the next year.

Step One

Take some time out in a quiet place to reflect on your intentions for the year ahead.

Like the Lo Shu Grid, there are nine areas on your manifestation board, and they are:

Fame & Illumination
Relationships
Creativity/Children
Helpful People
Career
Wealth/Knowledge
Romance & Ancestry
Good Fortune
Well-being

Step Two

Decide how you want to put your manifestation board together. If you do it digitally, a tool like Canva and your laptop may be all you need. If you're going to make a hard copy, then get everything you're going to need—corkboard, scissors, glue or tape, magazines, coloured pens, coloured paper, cut-out affirmations you love, personal photos of yourself or people you would like to bring into your life.

Step Three

When looking for inspiration, look for images representing what you want and that give you a positive feeling. Find quotes and symbols that feel right for you to help you achieve your goals. Remember, you can put more than one image in each area.

Step Four

It's time to put your board together now. I recommend playing uplifting music to add to the positive energy going into your board and to put you in the right frame of mind to visualise you achieving your goals. American rock star Pink is my music of choice.

Top Row, Left-hand Side Is Good Fortune

Decide what Good Fortune would look like to you in the next year. Find words, pictures, quotes, and anything else that represents Good Fortune for you. Aligning that in the right area for the year ahead will inspire you to attract it into your life.

Top Row, Middle Square Is Fame/Illumination

Here put images of red carpets or famous people who represent success and fame to you. I have a picture of a red carpet because I visualise myself walking on it when I launch my book.

Top Row, Right-hand Side Is Relationships

If you have a partner, put pictures of the two of you together, looking happy and relaxed. Symbols also work here—hearts and other things representing love to you, preferably in pairs. Don't put pictures of the two of you with anyone else in this space. You do not want a third person in your relationship. If you are looking for love, place two hearts together or other symbols of love. You'll know what represents love to you.

Middle Row, Left-hand Side Is Romance/Ancestry

As you know, I also call this the dustbin area. You can put whatever you want that doesn't seem to fit into the other eight areas of your grid.

One year I put in a Range Rover Evoque in grey. We talk a lot about action, but here is one example of putting this into practice. After putting a picture of my dream car on my manifestation board, I chose an auspicious day to look for one. There she was, abandoned at the back of a showroom garage. I insisted that was the one I wanted. The salesman tried to show others, but my partner Roger said, 'No, that's the one she wants. There will be no changing her mind.' They moved the other cars to get her out. I sat in the seat and knew immediately it was perfect for me.

Middle Row, Centre Square Is Well-being

This area can be harder for some people. I recommend using images, symbols, and words representing calm, quiet, tranquillity, and well-being for you. Anything that means quiet time and relaxing will work here.

Middle Row, Right-hand Side Is Creativity/Children

This area can be about children and other creations. If you want to have children, this is a great place to put images and symbols representing babies and children. Elephants with their babies are great imagery if this is your goal. You can also put pictures of your children in this area. If you have goals relating to your creativity, this is the place to put images and symbols to represent them, whether painting, pottery, books, or poetry. I have a picture of a woman waving a wand over a book to help me write my book.

Bottom Row, Left-hand Side Is Wealth/Knowledge

If wealth is about money and income to you, you can write yourself a check for £100k (or more) and pin it in this area. Wealth imagery and symbols are good here. Colour can also really help, particularly red and gold. If you are training or studying and want to succeed in obtaining more knowledge, then use images of books representing the subject you're studying. These are only ideas. It's important you put something in these areas that feels right to you.

Bottom Row, Centre Square Is Career/New Beginnings

This is one of my favourite areas to work on for the year ahead. Ask yourself what you want to happen in your career. Do you want a promotion, to change jobs, to start a business, or get a pay rise? Do you want to move, travel, or buy a house? You might ask yourself what direction you want your career to take. Pick images and symbols representing this change for you, and put them here.

Bottom Row, Right-hand Side Is Helpful People

Who inspires you to achieve what you want to achieve? Who can help you get where you want to go? Your boss, a mentor, or someone who has succeeded in your area would all fit here. Who can help teach you what you need to know? Who would you like to work with in the next year? Pick symbols and images of people who could help you get to where you want to go to attract them into your life. Inspirational quotes also work here, particularly if they're from people who represent success in your field.

I've even appeared on some of my client's manifestation boards as someone who can help them navigate their way through the next year. Check out the chart at the end of this chapter to see a visual display of the areas for your manifestation board.

Ensure you enjoy making your board. The energy you put into your board allows the magic to happen!

After you have created your Feng Shui Manifestation Board, I want you to look out for signposts. What do I mean by signposts?

It won't surprise you to know that I am a great believer in meaningful coincidences that appear to be more than random chance occurrences. Signs that appear to show us the way towards what we're aiming for or to remind us that we are on the right path.

For me, synchronicity is about things that happen and are connected in a meaningful way. They can feel like coincidences, but I do not believe in coincidences, especially when they relate directly to something that happens at exactly the right time and in exactly the right place.

Let me give you an example. A lovely friend of mine was all set to buy a shop, but there were constant obstacles getting in her way. Nothing was going smoothly, and there were delays. Just as she was about to give up on the idea, the shop next door came up for rent. We talked about it. She took advice from her mum and ended up pulling out of the first shop she had wanted. Happily, she had the keys to her new shop within six weeks. She was in the right place and at the right time, and ended up in the shop she was meant to have.

I'm going to leave this section with this thought. My manifestation boards have included images of books, and success signs, like the red carpet. This is my third book.

Energy for Success

Harnessing your personal energy enhances your goals and attracts positive outcomes. You can do this by cultivating a positive mindset, believing in yourself, changing your attitude when confronted by blocks, and flipping a negative mindset into a positive one to ensure success.

You need to align your personal goals and actions with your values and purpose in life. When they are aligned, you can achieve extraordinary success. Using your energy for things you don't believe in won't work. Don't waste your time or energy on anything that feels wrong; it's not worth it. If it doesn't feel right, it probably isn't.

I was working with a client with grand ambitions and money to spend. A lot was going on in his personal life, and the phone would ring as soon as I had him focused on work. His partner would ring, and because they had a toxic relationship, he would lose focus.

I pointed out the pattern to him, and he began to see that his partner could be an energy vampire. When we sorted out the drain on his energy, he grew from strength to strength. Think about your friends, family, and colleagues. Can you see a pattern like my client's? If so, you may need to consider cutting that person out of your life and releasing them with love. That will remove draining and negative energy so that you can grow.

You must look after your energy as well. You can use manifestation, mindset, affirmations, gratitude, and action, but your energy will deplete if you're not looking after yourself physically, mentally, and emotionally. Regular exercise, proper nutrition, enough good quality sleep, and self-care are all great ideas, but ultimately you know what you need.

Stress management is a great idea. It's easy to say but not that easy to do. Yoga, Tai Chi, Pilates, Reflexology, Reiki, Acupuncture, and other alternative therapies can help you manage your stress and keep your positive energy up. It's hard for anyone to stay positive when they're exhausted.

Think of your body as a battery; when it runs out, it needs recharging or refilling; if we don't do that, it simply won't work. Some people only fill that battery up to a certain level to keep moving, so they always run out of energy. You need to get to the optimum level before you take on large projects that are important to you. Suppose you've only got half of your energy. In that case, the most likely outcome is that you'll only achieve half of what you want and perhaps less if you struggle to maintain your positivity. Anything worth having is worth putting your all into.

How Can You Use Energy for Success?

I used energy successfully with a client who was always tired and very depressed. She was struggling to concentrate on anything, and constantly suffered from headaches.

Her house was full of clutter, and it had literally overwhelmed her. Her windows needed cleaning, and her front door needed painting. My brief from her was to help her feel better and to help shift some of her stuck and stagnant energy. How did I help her shift her energy?

To explain this clearly, I'm going to introduce you to a concept I use. Our homes are related to parts of our bodies:

Roof, attic, and loft are our heads.
Windows are our eyes.
The front door is our mouth; and
The centre of our homes is our stomach.

My client's loft was full. She had five old TVs, some of which didn't even work. She had her mother's belongings inherited by her when her mum had passed. She was clearly still emotionally attached to them and felt guilty about letting her mum go. All of those things held her late mother's energy.

Decluttering can be a hard thing to do by yourself, so I asked her to get her friends together and make a day of clearing. Luckily, she had a whole group of friends who wanted to help. They did charity shop and dump runs to get rid of everything she no longer needed or wanted. I asked her to burn sage while she was decluttering to enhance her own Chi and add positive energy to the house.

A month later, I visited her, and the change in her energy was huge. It felt like she was 200% more energetic, and there was a definite spring in her step. She seemed like a different person.

Energy gets stuck, and if you move it, then change will begin.

Visualisation

Visualisation is much the same as mindset. It helps you to manifest and use your personal energy in a way that will support your goals. By visualising your end goal, you enhance and attract positive outcomes.

For me:

Mindset is about thinking,
Manifesting is about words with actions, and
Visualisation is about seeing and dreaming.

They help and support each other. The key to using visualisation successfully is being super clear on what you want. Don't let any negative thoughts take over. One way to do this is to write down what you want first and then focus on it.

Ask yourself what is motivating you in this direction. Why do you want this end result? Motivation is a huge tool to use. Your motivation might be to give your child the best possible life you can, you may want your parents to be proud of you, or it might be a long-held dream just for yourself.

One key factor when visualising is to think of the result rather than the journey to get to the outcome. The clearer the image in your head of what you're aiming for, the more likely you will achieve it. This goes for feeling it as well. How will it feel when you accomplish this long-held goal? Imagine it's already happened—what emotions are you experiencing?

When you visualise, it needs to align with your values and beliefs, and you need to apply your positive mindset to it as well. You could unknowingly attract negative energy if you're not in the right frame of mind. This is where feeling your best emotionally and physically can contribute.

Once you've started visualising, make sure you recharge and rejuvenate overnight, and then go through the visualisation process again three more times. Try to visualise the end outcome more vividly each time.

How Does Visualisation Work with Feng Shui?

Visualisation can be very powerful when using Feng Shui in your home or office. While decluttering and cleaning, visualisation will complement your action because it can enhance your focus.

I used this in a consultation for a client called Lorna. She wanted a new job. The North of her home was cluttered; we spoke about her aspirations for her career. She loved the company she worked with but didn't feel suited to her position.

I went through her Bazi reading. A Bazi reading is drawn up from your date of birth (and time of birth if you have that). Sure enough, her Bazi showed that she should be working in marketing, not sales. I asked her to visualise her company, the marketing department she wanted to work in and to picture herself with her new colleagues. She found this particularly easy because she knew them all.

Lorna played music in the North of her home as she decluttered, cleaned, and repainted the area blue. She visualised herself picking up the phone and talking to people in her new role in marketing.

A month later she rang me and said a vacancy had come up and she applied for it. Did she get the job? Of course, she did.

Take Action!

Manifestation boards are powerful tools that work alongside mindset, manifestation, and visualisation. But none of this is going to happen if you don't act towards your goals. My Range Rover wasn't just going to appear in my driveway at home. I had to go and look for it. If you want your dream job, you can't just manifest or visualise it coming to you—you need to apply for it, or if it's not been advertised, contact the organisation you want to work with.

To be a doctor, you must study, get good grades, and apply for a medical degree. It won't just happen because you stick a picture on your wall. Both need to happen Nobody can win the lotto without buying a ticket. Everything else in life is the same. Luck and opportunities happen, but you need to be in the right place at the right time. There's no point hanging around a hospital hoping someone offers you a job if you haven't got the qualifications, experience, and skills. The good news is that you can make all that happen by taking the right actions.

What actions are you going to take to align yourself with your intentions? The thought is not the action. If you don't act, it doesn't matter what else you do; it won't happen. With

Feng Shui, setting your intention, manifesting, visualising, and taking action, you will attract abundance into your life.

We've covered the power of mindset and manifestation and how they work with Feng Shui; in the next chapter, I will share with you some of my success stories so you can see how everything you've read works in practice.

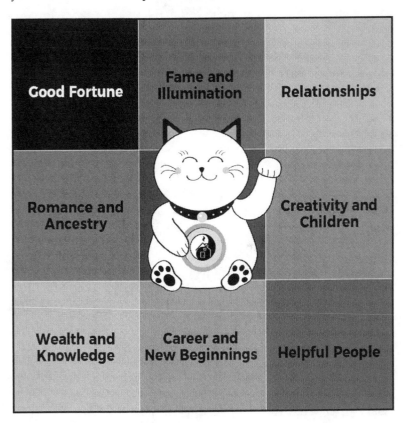

Chapter Eleven

Feng Shui in Action

I wanted to show you how the knowledge and experience I've shared in this book are used in practice to help my clients. You'll get a sense of how it can help you activate abundance in your own life.

To make it more accessible, I've included stories from eight of the nine areas of our homes and offices. As you know, I don't recommend activating the centre of our homes, so I haven't included it here. It will help your well-being if you simply keep it clean and clear.

North – Belinda's Story

I met Belinda at a networking lunch. We hit it off immediately. Back then, she was employed full-time, but she'd seen a gap in the market and wanted to set up her own business. She wanted to open an aesthetics clinic.

She would need to reduce her working hours to make time to launch the business. She had a very supportive husband, but they had two kids, and she knew she was putting the family's finances on the line.

When Belinda called me for a consultation, she admitted that she knew nothing about Feng Shui. But she'd done her homework and was up for giving it a go to achieve her goals. I asked her what she wanted to earn, and she was very clear that her goal was £100k a year. It was ambitious given she was in her first year of business, having started from nothing, but Belinda is a strong woman and works hard to achieve what she wants. The goal itself was clear, and she was realistic about her capacity to achieve it.

In that first year, 2010, we placed a water feature (fish tank) at the North of her clinic and another outside in the East. I recommended that she keep her clients' files in the North-West, the area of helpful people, where the wealth star fell that year.

I go back to Belinda's clinic every year, and we change the water features according to the annual Flying Stars. I do a reading for her so she knows what's coming up for her throughout the coming year. She can plan around her wealth months and make sure she goes on holidays during her clash months. I include her husband and two boys in the reading to get the complete picture for the whole family.

The Outcome:
Belinda has long since achieved her initial £100k goal and is close to achieving £300k per year. She is opening her first accredited school in laser treatments in November this year.

My readings and annual Feng Shui consultation based on the annual Flying Stars have given her the information she needed to maximise her business income, but equally, the key to her success was that she has worked hard and taken action to achieve her goals.

North-East – Sebastian's Story

Julie called me in to help her 11-year-old son Sebastian. She'd heard about me through one of her friends. He was intelligent but was struggling at school. He was having trouble concentrating and had become the class clown. He'd reached the age where he really needed to knuckle down to his studies.

He loved attention from his family, friends, and peers. That meant he spent a lot of time focused on pleasing other people and never thought about what he wanted to achieve for himself. His room was untidy, but that's not unusual for a boy of that age.

Sebastian was born in the year of the Rooster and the month of the Rabbit, which caused an internal clash. This meant he needed more confidence and questioned every decision he made. He was born under the 3 Jade Wood Star, so he had amazing career prospects. He could easily end up a solicitor, barrister or even a judge.

There were two areas I focused on to help Sebastian. I noticed in his bedroom that the top of his head was facing South. That meant he wasn't getting much sleep. I moved his bed position, so the top of his head faced North and changed his bed linen colour to blue. Blue is a great colour for the North area of our homes.

The second area was the North-East which is about knowledge and wealth. Wealth wasn't relevant to Sebastian at his young age, so I focused on knowledge and study. I placed him in the North-East with his back to the wall and his desk facing the door. I asked Julie to get him a red book to write in and a load of coloured pens. Roosters love glittery, colourful stuff, even the boys.

Based on his date of birth, I knew that his best times to study were 07.00–09.00 and again at 17.00–19.00. I recommended that he study for two hours a day for six days a week within those times.

The Outcome:
Sebastian settled down to his study and even started to enjoy it in his new auspicious space in the North-East. Julie is thrilled with his amazing school results. He is well and truly back on track. Now he enjoys studying, and as his homework time is ringfenced, Julie doesn't have to worry or nag him about it.

East – Jackie's Story

I was called in to consult with Jackie. She was estranged from her family and very lonely. When Jackie was 13 years old, her mother, Ruth, had fallen out with her sister, Mabel. Ruth had moved 300 miles away, and Jackie was never allowed to contact Mabel's twin daughters and younger son. Jackie was an only child, so her cousins had been very important to her. To make matters worse, Ruth would never explain what had caused the argument. By the time Jackie contacted me, Ruth and Mabel had passed.

Jackie was born in the year, month, and day of the Rabbit. Family is incredibly important to Rabbits, but with all of that Rabbit influence — it was everything to Jackie.

The East was the most important area to activate because it's all about ancestry. The element for this space is wood, and the supporting element is water. I suggested she place a water feature outside her front door because it faces the East. It was very convenient that her door faced East because it was that door I needed her cousins to walk through. I asked her to paint it blue, and she placed two citrus trees on either side.

I also recommended that she put together a manifestation board with pictures of her, her cousins, Ruth, and Mabel. Once she'd done that, I gave her an auspicious date to contact her cousins. She found one of her cousins through Facebook. However, now was when she needed to act and contact her cousin. She rang me to say she was nervous about doing it. I told her to go for it.

The Outcome:
Three months later, Jackie sent me a picture of herself with her cousins in a garden centre having a coffee. They all had huge smiles on their faces. Job done!

South-East – Claudie's Story

One of my favourite clients was a lady called Claudie. When I first met Claudie at her home, I felt like I'd been transported back in time because she was so glamorous.

Claudie is a Horse in Chinese Astrology, and she was born under the 8 White Earth Star, which meant money would never be a problem. I needed to know whether she used her wealth star well.

I always do my clients' charts based on their dates of birth before I meet them. They tell me so much about the person who has requested the consultation. Her chart told me that Claudie was a hoarder. I knew that I would be going into a house full of clutter. That also meant that she had trouble making decisions.

Her house was full of expensive soft furnishings, paintings, and heavy oak furniture. It felt dark and musty. We sat in the drawing room, where a maid brought in coffee and tea. I felt like I'd been transported to an earlier century.

I asked Claudie what she wanted from the consultation. What was it that she wanted to change? Her response was, 'Everything. I feel like I'm in prison.' I hadn't expected that answer. She appeared to have everything, but it was clear that wealth and all the trappings were not making her happy.

She told me she wanted to travel but felt like the house was holding her back. Yet she had nothing keeping her there. She didn't even have pets.

We talked for hours before I assessed her home. As I expected, it was overflowing with books and memorabilia. She'd inherited such a lot from her ancestors.

The area that needed changing became clear when I went into the South-East of her home. This space is all about good fortune and legal matters. I asked her if any legal issues were hanging over her head. She told me she had her mother's home and her portfolio of houses to sell, with more wealth coming her way.

The South-East was full of heavy furniture and felt drab. It wasn't a comfortable place to spend time. Clearly, this was the area I needed to help her activate for the change she wanted.

I advised her to sell everything in the room or put it into storage. We needed a blank canvas to get positive energy moving. She was able to get people to help her to do this. I recommended she open the windows daily to bring positive Chi from outside.

Once everything was gone, we bought her a lighter desk. We introduced a rich red into the room and put a piano in the corner because she loved to play. It became a space she wanted to spend time in.

The Outcome:
She rang me a few months later and asked me to visit her. As soon as she opened the door, I could see the change in her. She looked so happy and had booked her first cruise. She told me that she was planning to declutter the house. I advised her to take on one room at a time. If people take on too much at once, it can become overwhelming, and they may give up.

South – Jack's Story

My client Jack was a famous actor. He'd been in a number of films. He'd met me when he'd been married to another of my clients. He'd seen what Feng Shui had done for her career, so he consulted me.

Jack wanted to reignite his career as it had taken a downturn. He'd had a great manager, but the public had lost interest in him because of his messy divorce. I asked him what he would like. He said he'd love to appear on a reality TV show. He was keen to do something outside of his comfort zone.

He was born in the year of the Tiger and under the 9 Purple Star, which means he's a go-getter and can manifest his dreams.

I located the South of his home, which is all about fame. He was fortunate that his front door opened on the South. I recommended that he painted the front door red and put money plants outside on either side of the entrance.

We placed movie posters in the hallway and framed awards he'd won. We also put up a manifestation board with films and TV shows he'd like to be in. We added reality shows that he felt would get him public attention, where he could change their opinion of him after his very public divorce.

We placed a water feature in the North of his home in the garden to bring in new beginnings and opportunities.

The Outcome:
He was invited to star in a reality show a year after my consultations. Although he didn't enjoy being put in a coffin and covered in snakes, people started falling in love with him again and forgot about his messy divorce. He went on to have his own reality show, which ran for two seasons and then got the starring role he'd been waiting for.

South-West – Gracie's Story

Gracie was in her 50s when she contacted me. She was a widow. She and her husband had been school sweethearts. They'd been married for 20 years when she lost him to cancer. She'd been alone for about ten years when she called me in. She felt she'd lost the love of her life and didn't feel she could go out with someone else. But she was only in her 50s, and her family and friends were pushing her to move on. She was full of life and looked so much younger than she was.

When I did her chart, I discovered her Peach Blossom star was Rooster: in Chinese Astrology the term 'Peach Blossom' is linked to a person's attractiveness and charm. If you have this in your chart you are a magnet for others because your natural charisma draws people to you.

It was clear what she needed to do, but I knew it would be daunting for her. She needed to remove all the clutter and get rid of his clothes, aside from anything that held special memories. I asked her to play music while she cleared out the room. Once she'd done that, she needed to paint the back of the wardrobe red.

Using the knowledge that her peach blossom star was Rooster, we activated the West of her home to bring a new lover into her life. We created a manifestation board of everything she wants in a new partner. The most important point was that he would understand her love for her deceased husband.

Gracie loved nature and wildlife, so we placed a bird bath in the North of her garden to attract more birds, which made her very happy.

The Outcome:
Three months later, I got a call from Gracie. She'd been in her local supermarket and ran into a guy she'd gone to school with. He'd lost his wife to the same disease that had taken her husband. They were dating and taking it very slowly, which was perfect for her.

West – Chrissy and Brian's Story

I was called in to consult with Chrissy and Brian, who were struggling to have a baby. They'd been together since university and had spent years pursuing their careers, hobbies, and travelling. When they decided to start a family, they assumed it would be easy. It was not. Eventually, they became disillusioned. They had everything they wanted except a baby. They contacted me because I have had a lot of success helping people conceive babies, thanks to being able to determine auspicious times and using Feng Shui.

Chrissy is a Yin Goat, and Brian is a Yang Horse. This means that Chrissy is feminine and incredibly gentle, whereas Brian is robust, outspoken and a bit bombastic. Chrissy was born under the 6 White Star and Brian under the 7 Red Star, which is a very interesting combination to work with. The 6 White Star is all about helpful people, and the 7 Red Star is about a person getting what they want and loving to party.

Brian was not happy about consulting me. Chrissy persevered and they finally agreed to bring me in, but he was far from a believer. I talked to them about their extended family dynamics, and it became clear that Brian didn't get along with his family, so he relied on his wife a lot for her support.

I concentrated on the West of their home because that's the area where creativity and children are based. In their case, the West was a spare room used to store junk. I advised them to declutter the space, paint it white and move their bed in there with the tops of their heads facing West when they slept. Then I determined the most auspicious dates for them to do what needed to be done to make a baby.

The Outcome:
Three months later, Chrissy contacted me on FaceTime and said, 'Guess what, Janine, I'm pregnant.' Brian popped his head over Chrissy's shoulder and said, 'Sorry for not believing.'

North-West – Tabitha
Tabitha called me in because she was lonely. When I arrived at her home in Nottingham, I found a small, petite lady with a very orderly, spotless house. I noticed that there was no TV, radio, or anything that would make a noise. There were no pictures on her walls and nothing on her kitchen worktops other than a kettle.

I asked her if she liked animals. She said she loved them but couldn't have a pet because it would make a mess.

When I did her chart, I understood why she had said that. Tabitha is a Snake born in the month of the Pig. That told me she's super intelligent but struggles with OCD. She has a self-clash in her chart with the Snake and the Pig, so I had to take tiny steps to help her improve her lifestyle.

Obviously, we would need to work in the North-West of her home, which is about helpful people. I needed to bring people into her life who would support her on her journey.

I asked her to make a manifestation board. I told her it was okay to use black and white images, so she wasn't confronted by too much colour. We put the picture inside one of the cupboards in the North-West where she kept her tea, so she would see it whenever she made a cuppa. I knew there was no point in having it on show. It would just trigger her.

After assessing her home, I recommended that she volunteer at her local animal sanctuary. So, what has that got to do with Feng Shui? It's my job to be a detective and use my skills and experience to work out what is blocking people from achieving the life they want. In Tabitha's case, she was lonely. She obviously loved animals rather than people, but that's another story.

Initially, I checked in with Tabitha every few weeks to see how she was getting on. We enjoyed our chats, and she said how much she looked forward to talking to me.

The Outcome:
Tabitha volunteered at the local animal sanctuary and adopted two elderly cats, which was so lovely to hear for both her and the cats. She isn't lonely anymore.

Conclusion

I've spent years as a Feng Shui consultant helping people create the lives they truly want. Ultimately, we all want abundant lives, whatever that means to each of us. Feng Shui has been around for thousands of years, and can help activate and create positive energy in your home and office to impact your life significantly.

In this book, I've shown you the tools you can use to improve your life and what not to do if you want to avoid stagnating or attracting negative energy. By the time you've reached here, you will have taken the time to work out what areas of your life you most want to improve. You now have the information you need to enhance energy flow in your home and bring your dreams alive.

You need to mix this knowledge with a healthy dose of positive thinking, optimism, and an active mindset. Manifesting and visualising your ideal outcome will help. But ultimately, you must act. You need to put in place the things you've learned here.

Don't overload yourself. Pick the three most important areas to you. Then start taking action in the key space first. Once you see changes there, you will be impatient to start in the other areas. But my advice is to give one space your full attention. Spreading your efforts may lead to your feeling overwhelmed, and you could give up. Once you've reached your goals in one area, you'll be motivated to move on to another.

My abundance formula is:

Dream + Feng Shui Knowledge + Positive Mindset and Manifestation + Action = Abundance.

None of these are dispensable. You need all of them to create the life you really want. There's no point moving the furniture around and putting together a manifestation board without taking action to move forward with your primary goal.

Better still, as the annual Flying Stars change position every year, you know what to do to take full advantage of them, according to your priorities. December is a great time to think about your main goals for the coming year, then put the changes in place in February or after the Chinese New Year; by doing this you can expect a positive year ahead.

Onwards and upwards, with this knowledge and these tools, may your life be the abundant one you have always dreamed of.

Flying Stars Cheat Sheet

I thought I would write a cheat sheet for the Flying Stars, because yes, it is complicated. While I know there will be some advanced Feng Shui people studying these charts and enjoying the complexity of them, some of you will just be looking for the auspicious/favourable areas to enhance each year.

You may notice that you might not be able to use wealth, or one of the other auspicious life houses, every year as the Chinese animal of the year may clash with the Star in a particular area. For example, the Chinese Animal for 2032 is the Rat and the Wealth Star is in the South which is a clash for the Horse. Please refer to previous chapters to remind yourself of information relating to clashes.

Never activate the wealth star if it falls in the centre of the grid as the 5 Yellow Star lives there permanently, and if activated you will have a roller coaster of a year with your finances.

In fact, don't activate any auspicious numbers, i.e. 1, 9, 4, 6, and 8, even if they are in the centre. The centre of your house needs to be kept quiet.

In the next few pages are the locations of the auspicious Stars for years 2024–2049, including grids showing the Stars which always reside in each area along with the annual Flying Stars which have flown in for the year:

2024 Wood Dragon
North Wealth
North-East Wealth & Helpful People
East New Beginnings/Career
South-West Manifesting/Fame

2025 Wood Snake
East Fame & Manifest

South-East New Beginnings & Career
South Helpful People
South-West Wealth
West Good Fortune

2026 Fire Horse
East Wealth
South-East Manifest & Fame
North-East Good Fortune

2027 Fire Goat
North-West New Beginnings & Career
South-West Helpful People
South Good Fortune
South-East Wealth

2028 Earth Monkey
East Helpful People
West New Beginnings & Career
North Good Fortune
North-West Manifest & Fame

2029 Earth Rooster
South-East Helpful People
South-West Good Fortune
West Manifest/Fame
North-East New Beginnings & Career
North-West Wealth

2030 Metal Dog
South New Beginnings & Career
East Good Fortune
West Wealth
North-East Manifest & Fame

2031 Metal Pig
South Manifest & Fame
North-East Wealth
North New Beginnings & Fame
North-West Helpful People

2032 Water Rat
South-West New Beginnings & Career
West Helpful People
North Manifest & Fame

2033 Water Ox
North Wealth
North-East Wealth & Helpful People
East New Beginnings/Career
North-West Good Fortune

2034 Wood Tiger
East Fame & Manifest
South-East New Beginnings & Career
South Helpful People
West Good Fortune

2035 Wood Rabbit
East Wealth
South-East Manifest & Fame
North-East Good Fortune
North Helpful People

2036 Fire Dragon
South-West Helpful People
South Good Fortune
South-East Wealth

2037 Fire Snake
East Helpful People
West New Beginnings & Career
North Good Fortune

2038 Earth Horse
South-East Helpful People
South-West Good Fortune
West Manifest/Fame
North-East New Beginnings & Career
North-West Wealth

2039 Earth Goat
South New Beginnings & Career
East Good Fortune
West Wealth
North-East Manifest & Fame

2040 Metal Monkey
South Manifest & Fame
North New Beginnings & Fame
North-West Helpful People
South-East Good Fortune

2041 Metal Rooster
South-West New Beginnings & Career
West Helpful People
North Manifest & Fame
South Wealth

2042 Water Dog
North Wealth

North-East Wealth & Helpful People
East New Beginnings/Career
North-West Good Fortune

2043 Water Pig
East Fame & Manifest
South Helpful People
South-West Wealth
West Good Fortune

2044 Wood Rat
East Wealth
South-East Manifest & Fame
North-East New Beginnings & Career
North Helpful People

2045 Wood Ox
North-West New Beginnings & Career
South-West Helpful People
South Good Fortune
South-East Wealth

2046 Fire Tiger
East Helpful People
West New Beginnings & Career
North Good Fortune
North-West Manifest & Fame

2047 Fire Rabbit
South-East Helpful People
South-West Good Fortune
North-East New Beginnings & Career
North-West Wealth

2048 Earth Dragon
South New Beginnings & Career
East Good Fortune
West Wealth
North-East Manifest & Fame

2049 Earth Snake
South Manifest & Fame
North-East Wealth
North New Beginnings & Fame

Janine Lowe
Flying Star

2023

South East	South	South West
4	9	2
East	Health	West
3	5	7
North East	North	North West
8	1	6

2024

South East	South	South West
4	9	2
East	Health	West
3	5	7
North East	North	North West
8	1	6

2025

South East	South	South West
4	9	2
East	Health	West
3	5	7
North East	North	North West
8	1	6

2026

South East	South	South West
4	9	2
East	Health	West
3	5	7
North East	North	North West
8	1	6

2027

South East	South	South West
4	9	2
East	Health	West
3	5	7
North East	North	North West
8	1	6

2028

South East	South	South West
4	9	2
East	Health	West
3	5	7
North East	North	North West
8	1	6

2029

South East	South	South West
4	9	2
East	Health	West
3	5	7
North East	North	North West
8	1	6

2030

South East	South	South West
4	9	2
East	Health	West
3	5	7
North East	North	North West
8	1	6

2031

South East	South	South West
4	9	2
East	Health	West
3	5	7
North East	North	North West
8	1	6

Janine Lowe

Flying Star

2032

South East	South	South West
4 ₃	9 ₈	2 ₁
East	**Health**	**West**
3 ₂	5 ₄	7 ₆
North East	**North**	**North West**
8 ₇	1 ₉	6 ₅

2033

South East	South	South West
4 ₂	9 ₇	2 ₉
East	**Health**	**West**
3 ₁	5 ₃	7 ₅
North East	**North**	**North West**
8 ₆	1 ₈	6 ₄

2034

South East	South	South West
4 ₁	9 ₆	2 ₈
East	**Health**	**West**
3 ₉	5 ₂	7 ₄
North East	**North**	**North West**
8 ₅	1 ₇	6

2035

South East	South	South West
4 ₉	9 ₅	2 ₇
East	**Health**	**West**
3 ₈	5 ₁	7 ₃
North East	**North**	**North West**
8 ₄	1 ₆	6 ₂

2036

South East	South	South West
4 ₈	9 ₄	2 ₆
East	**Health**	**West**
3 ₇	5 ₉	7 ₂
North East	**North**	**North West**
8 ₃	1 ₅	6 ₁

2037

South East	South	South West
4 ₇	9 ₃	2 ₅
East	**Health**	**West**
3 ₆	5 ₈	7 ₁
North East	**North**	**North West**
8 ₂	1 ₄	6 ₉

2038

South East	South	South West
4 ₆	9 ₂	2 ₄
East	**Health**	**West**
3 ₅	5 ₇	7 ₉
North East	**North**	**North West**
8 ₁	1 ₃	6 ₈

2039

South East	South	South West
4 ₅	9 ₁	2 ₃
East	**Health**	**West**
3 ₄	5 ₆	7 ₈
North East	**North**	**North West**
8 ₉	1 ₂	6 ₇

2040

South East	South	South West
4 ₄	9 ₉	2 ₂
East	**Health**	**West**
3 ₃	5 ₅	7 ₇
North East	**North**	**North West**
8 ₈	1 ₁	6 ₆

Janine Lowe
Flying Star

2041

South East	South	South West
4	9	2
East	Health	West
3	5	7
North East	North	North West
8	1	6

2042

South East	South	South West
4	9	2
East	Health	West
3	5	7
North East	North	North West
8	1	6

2043

South East	South	South West
4	9	2
East	Health	West
3	5	7
North East	North	North West
8	1	6

2044

South East	South	South West
4	9	2
East	Health	West
3	5	7
North East	North	North West
8	1	6

2045

South East	South	South West
4	9	2
East	Health	West
3	5	7
North East	North	North West
8	1	6

2046

South East	South	South West
4	9	2
East	Health	West
3	5	7
North East	North	North West
8	1	6

2047

South East	South	South West
4	9	2
East	Health	West
3	5	7
North East	North	North West
8	1	6

2048

South East	South	South West
4	9	2
East	Health	West
3	5	7
North East	North	North West
8	1	6

2049

South East	South	South West
4	9	2
East	Health	West
3	5	7
North East	North	North West
8	1	6

O-BOOKS

SPIRITUALITY

O is a symbol of the world, of oneness and unity; this eye
represents knowledge and insight. We publish titles on general
spirituality and living a spiritual life. We aim to inform and
help you on your own journey in this life.
If you have enjoyed this book, why not tell other readers
by posting a review on your preferred book site?

Recent bestsellers from O-Books are:

Heart of Tantric Sex
Diana Richardson
Revealing Eastern secrets of deep love and
intimacy to Western couples.
Paperback: 978-1-90381-637-0 ebook: 978-1-84694-637-0

Crystal Prescriptions
The A-Z guide to over 1,200 symptoms and their healing crystals
Judy Hall
The first in the popular series of eight books, this handy
little guide is packed as tight as a pill bottle with
crystal remedies for ailments.
Paperback: 978-1-90504-740-6 ebook: 978-1-84694-629-5

Shine On
David Ditchfield and J S Jones
What if the after effects of a near-death experience were undeniable? What if a person could suddenly produce high-quality paintings of the afterlife, or if they acquired the ability to compose classical symphonies? Meet: David Ditchfield.
Paperback: 978-1-78904-365-5 ebook: 978-1-78904-366-2

The Way of Reiki
The Inner Teachings of Mikao Usui
Frans Stiene
The roadmap for deepening your understanding of the system of Reiki and rediscovering your True Self.
Paperback: 978-1-78535-665-0 ebook: 978-1-78535-744-2

You Are Not Your Thoughts
Frances Trussell
The journey to a mindful way of being, for those who want to truly know the power of mindfulness.
Paperback: 978-1-78535-816-6 ebook: 978-1-78535-817-3

The Mysteries of the Twelfth Astrological House
Fallen Angels
Carmen Turner-Schott, MSW, LISW
Everyone wants to know more about the most misunderstood house in astrology — the twelfth astrological house.
Paperback: 978-1-78099-343-0 ebook: 978-1-78099-344-7

WhatsApps from Heaven
Louise Hamlin
An account of a bereavement and the extraordinary
signs — including WhatsApps — that a retired
law lecturer received from her deceased husband.
Paperback: 978-1-78904-947-3 ebook: 978-1-78904-948-0

The Holistic Guide to Your Health
& Wellbeing Today
Oliver Rolfe
A holistic guide to improving your complete health,
both inside and out.
Paperback: 978-1-78535-392-5 ebook: 978-1-78535-393-2

Cool Sex
Diana Richardson and Wendy Doeleman
For deeply satisfying sex, the real secret is to reduce the heat,
to cool down. Discover the empowerment and fulfilment
of sex with loving mindfulness.
Paperback: 978-1-78904-351-8 ebook: 978-1-78904-352-5

Creating Real Happiness A to Z
Stephani Grace
Creating Real Happiness A to Z will help you understand
the truth that you are not your ego
(conditioned self).
Paperback: 978-1-78904-951-0 ebook: 978-1-78904-952-7

A Colourful Dose of Optimism
Jules Standish
It's time for us to look on the bright side, by boosting
our mood and lifting our spirit, both in
our interiors, as well as in our closet.
Paperback: 978-1-78904-927-5 ebook: 978-1-78904-928-2

Readers of ebooks can buy or view any of these bestsellers by
clicking on the live link in the title. Most titles are published
in paperback and as an ebook. Paperbacks are available in
traditional bookshops. Both print and ebook formats are
available online.

Find more titles and sign up to our readers' newsletter at
www.o-books.com

Follow O-Books on Facebook at **O-Books**

For video content, author interviews and more, please subscribe to our YouTube channel:

O-BOOKS Presents

Follow us on social media for book news, promotions and more:

Facebook: O-Books

Instagram: @o_books_mbs

X: @obooks

Tik Tok: @ObooksMBS

www.o-books.com